T5-AGO-454

A PUBLICATION OF KAPPA DELTA PI
AN HONOR SOCIETY IN EDUCATION

—Blackstone Studios

WILLIAM CHANDLER BAGLEY, 1874–1946

A KAPPA DELTA PI PUBLICATION

WILLIAM CHANDLER BAGLEY

STALWART EDUCATOR

BY

I. L. KANDEL

PROFESSOR EMERITUS OF EDUCATION
TEACHERS COLLEGE, COLUMBIA UNIVERSITY
EMERITUS PROFESSOR OF AMERICAN STUDIES
UNIVERSITY OF MANCHESTER

BUREAU OF PUBLICATIONS

TEACHERS COLLEGE, COLUMBIA UNIVERSITY

NEW YORK, 1961

LIBRARY OF CONGRESS CATALOG CARD NUMBER: 61–7709

MANUFACTURED IN THE UNITED STATES OF AMERICA

EDITOR'S INTRODUCTION

IN PUBLISHING THIS BIOGRAPHY AND INTERPRETATION OF THE philosophy of William Chandler Bagley, Kappa Delta Pi, an Honor Society in Education, in its fiftieth-year celebration has two prime purposes: first, to recognize the man who was a key figure in its founding and in its continuous development into a leading American exponent of excellence in teachers and their professional preparation; and second, to preserve for educational professional workers the philosophy and record of the activities of a nationally and internationally recognized scholar who is accounted by many of his associates as the principal exponent over a period of many years of the development of high-grade professional preparation of teachers through his insistence upon thorough scholarship and high professional skill for teachers on all levels of education.

Dr. Bagley's contribution was made during a period of educational ferment in America when divergent philosophies of life and education were held and expressed. Under his espousal of the movement technically known as "essentialism" he took issue with some of the extreme positions which once were dominant in extreme cults of "progressivism." During the half-century of his professional service he insisted that the "cause of education at all levels" needed strong emphasis on up-grading.

Currently in American education there is a renewal of active and vigorous debate on the emphasis which should be given to differing aspects of education, again bringing into focus the conflicts that in the past have been so earnest and vigorous, such as the social aspects versus the individualistic, and the immediately practical and vocational versus the general, liberal, and basic. In the current debate the views of Dr. Bagley are pertinent and significant. It is to be deplored that there are not a greater number of definitive biographies of the leaders in educational thought during the last half century. Though Dr. Bagley's views were presented in many addresses, magazine articles, and books, it is only now that a full generalized analysis of his contributions is made in one source.

For this task no one is better qualified than Dr. Kandel. He is internationally known as one of today's great scholars in education. For many years he devoted himself to the field of comparative education. The Executive Council recognized his special fitness for making a major contribution when it commissioned him to write this biography. He was associated with Dr. Bagley on the Faculty of Teachers College, Columbia University, over a long period and was one of his close personal friends. Probably no one knew so well as he Bagley's philosophy, not only as it has been expressed in his books and magazine articles, but through personal contacts. Rarely have the biographer and the subject of the biography had so much in common; rarely has a biographer been so intimately acquainted with his subject and his inner thoughts; and rarely has a great educational philosopher had so competent and so understanding an interpreter.

The Society and the entire teaching profession are deeply in debt to Dr. Kandel for his masterly analysis of the educational philosophy of one of the truly great scholars in American educational history. It is with a sense of deep gratitude that Kappa Delta Pi recognizes the permanent record of Dr. Bagley's work as exhibited in this volume. It is a great biography by a great scholar, an interpretation which will add depth and understanding in the current debates in the field of education.

E. I. F. WILLIAMS, *Editor*
Kappa Delta Pi Publications

PREFACE

THE PREPARATION OF THIS VOLUME WAS COMMISSIONED BY the Executive Council of Kappa Delta Pi, a professional honor society of which Dr. William Chandler Bagley was one of the distinguished founders, and which will celebrate the Fiftieth Anniversary of its founding in 1961. The book is more than a tribute to Dr. Bagley's close association with the society from its initiation in 1911 until his death in 1946. It presents an account of the professional activities and contributions of an educator who, more than any other in his day, strove to maintain a balanced point of view in education in the midst of the constant bombardment of an increasing number of cure-alls and panaceas which he began to criticize as early as 1907. A staunch protagonist of the American tradition of education, he stressed the paramount importance of the professional preparation of teachers combined with thorough mastery of subject matter. He sought always to close the gap between those who stood for academic subjects and those who were responsible for professional subjects. Long before others began to realize the decline in the quality of secondary education, he frequently urged the value and importance of "exact and exacting studies" and deplored the relaxation of standards in high schools.

The subtitle of the book, "Stalwart Educator," is one that Dr. Bagley would have favored, for he objected to being referred to as traditional or conservative. He always lived up to his own interpretation of a stalwart educator as one who "makes systematic, orderly progress the central feature of his educational program."

The author expresses his indebtedness to the Executive Council of Kappa Delta Pi for the opportunity to pay homage to the memory of an old friend and colleague. To Dr. E. I. F. Williams he is grateful for his encouragement in this and other ventures associated with Kappa Delta Pi. He is happy to acknowledge the helpfulness of Dr. John W. Tietz in giving him the opportunity to check his bibliography of Dr. Bagley's writings with his own. And finally, he is indebted to Miss Clara Esther Derring of the Library of Teachers College, Columbia University, for facilitating for the author the loan of the periodical literature to which Dr. Bagley contributed so extensively, and to Miss Katherine M. Gilroy of the Bureau of Publications, Teachers College, for her care and skill in seeing the work through the press.

I.L.K.

CONTENTS

WILLIAM CHANDLER BAGLEY

STALWART EDUCATOR

CHAPTER 1

FROM RURAL SCHOOL TEACHING TO EDUCATIONAL LEADERSHIP

TO WRITE THE BIOGRAPHY OF WILLIAM CHANDLER BAGLEY is virtually to write the history of American education in the first half of the twentieth century. His name may not be associated, as he himself somewhat quizzically remarked on several occasions, with any particular innovation in educational theory, curriculum, or method of instruction, but there was hardly any educational problem that concerned elementary or secondary schools, the preparation and status of teachers, or the fundamental basis of American education as a social institution that he did not discuss constructively in his lectures and writings during the whole of his career. There was one innovation that he did claim when he was charged with criticizing every new proposal that was put forward in education. The innovation for which he fought in season and out of season was one that would put a competent and cultured teacher into every American classroom, an innovation that would do more for American education than would all the other proposed innovations put together.

Dr. Bagley came to be known in the latter part of his career as a traditionalist, if not as a reactionary, because of his continued and constant criticism of progressive education. Toward the end of his career he was referred to as an "essentialist," a term usually employed in derision by many who did not realize that he had begun to advocate rigorous attention to the "essentials" of education in one of the earliest of his many contributions to the literature of education. He refused, however, to be dubbed a traditionalist. Those who stood for the maintenance and preservation of the best in the tradition of education he would rather have called "stalwarts." As he suggested in *Education, Crime, and Social Progress,* "the stalwart makes systematic, orderly progress the central feature of his educational program. The Progressive recognizes system, if at all, only with averted face." He was a conservative in the best sense of the word, in the sense defined by President Theodore Roosevelt when he said that "the only true conservative is the man who resolutely sets his face toward the future." Bagley realized almost at the outset of his career that "in a complex process like education, it is always necessary to keep a clear perspective." It was this principle that guided him throughout his career and was the base from which he was ready to attack fads and innovations, "half-baked" reforms as he called them, that succeeded one another periodically. Because he believed that the teacher's best protection against their allurement was a firm and stable theoretical foundation, he sought from the start to formulate a sound educational theory which would serve the teacher in practice. His first book, *The Educative Process* (1905), dealt with principles rather than with details and methods in the belief that "not the least important element in the formation of effective ideals is substantial theory."

In the light of his subsequent career, it is interesting to recall that Bagley, like many others in his day, took up teaching as a steppingstone. He remained to become one of the distinguished members of the teaching profession because he found the work of teaching in a backwoods one-teacher school "interesting and challenging," and was inspired to look for sounder foundations on which to base education than those that existed in his day. He continued in this chosen task through his career and became the outstanding exponent and defender of the aims and ideals of

American education. At a time like the present, when there prevails a widespread demand for a return to the fundamentals of reading, writing, and arithmetic in the elementary schools, and for more serious attention to the study of foreign languages, mathematics, and science in the secondary schools, it is well to remember the aims and ideals for which Bagley stood throughout the more than forty years of his professional activity. He insisted day in and day out on the importance of the fundamentals for social and individual welfare and progress and as a basis for further education. At the secondary level he constantly referred to the "exact and exacting studies" to prepare youth to meet the social and national needs of their country and for the cultural development of the individual. He had an abiding faith in the value of these studies and saw the danger in the relaxation of standards in secondary education long before their immediate practical importance was realized because of the challenge from another country. He recognized, however, that the key to the educational situation is the well-prepared teacher and that no amount of "overhead," whether administrative or theoretical, could compensate for a poor teacher.

Bagley championed not only the cause of a sound preparation and a recognized professional status for teachers, but the right of every boy and girl to the best education appropriate to their capacities. More than anything he stood for freedom from cant in education. The role that he undertook from the start of his career he defined in the Preface of *Education, Crime, and Social Progress* when he wrote: "Our indicated task in the present very serious social situation, therefore, would seem to involve (1) an identification of the elements of weakness in American education and (2) an effort to replace these with elements of strength." A few pages later, after referring to the succession of innovations, he continued:

Although I have never had the good fortune myself to set on foot one of these new fashions in education, I am finding myself increasingly assuming a much humbler but perhaps in the end an equally significant function — namely, salvaging from the scrap-pile and preserving for the future the valuable elements which almost every one of these fashions represents — often, I admit, in microscopic amount, but worth saving none the less.

Bagley decided on his future role early in his career. Although there is ample evidence of this in his writings, there is virtually no information available about the early years of his life before he entered college. There is no mention of his parents except in the dedication of a book to them. All that is known about them is that they were born in Massachusetts. Bagley himself was born in Detroit, Michigan, on March 15, 1874, but, since he attended a public elementary school in Worcester, Massachusetts, it can only be assumed that the family moved back to New England. In the elementary school all his teachers were women until he reached the ninth grade which was taught by the principal, William H. Bartlett. Bagley retained a vivid memory of this man whom he includes in an article on "Some Master Teachers I Have Known."[1*] Bartlett impressed the boy because of his exceptionally well-controlled voice and his aversion to careless articulation and enunciation, qualities to which Bagley always paid considerable attention.

For his secondary education Bagley attended a high school in Detroit, which was still selective but offered three courses without Latin, of which two were accepted for college entrance. He drew attention to the choice of courses in his day to counter the perennial charge that the colleges had a stranglehold on the high school curriculum. At the same time he referred, in the article on "Latin from an Educationist's Point of View," to his ignorance of Latin as "a professional handicap."[2] In the high school none of the teachers seems to have impressed him as outstanding, but the principal, he recalled, was a refined and scholarly gentleman.

Except for the references to the character of the principals in the elementary and high schools that he attended, this period of his education apparently exercised no marked influence on Bagley's future development. It is to the next period, the college and university years, that one must look for influences that affected his outlook in his professional career. He entered the Michi-

*Numbers refer to items in References, pages 123–131.

gan Agricultural College, later the Michigan State College, in 1891, where he found teachers who impressed him with their personal qualities and with their scholarship. The instructor in chemistry, Roscoe C. Kedzie, Bagley was to describe nearly fifty years later as an exceptionally competent teacher and scholar. Kedzie lectured in a clear well-organized discourse that Bagley never heard surpassed in any college or university classroom. He was a schoolmaster of the old school, exact and exacting, but with a sense of humor, which seemed to Bagley to be an essential characteristic in most master teachers.

The professor of English, Howard Edwards, is described by Bagley as a courteous gentleman of unshaken integrity, kindly sympathy, and tolerance, "with a quizzical smile and twinkle." Edwards was an ideal teacher who made his subject "tingle with life." There was an element of adventure in his assignments which, combined with his artistry in teaching, made all his students see literature in a new light.

If these two instructors inspired Bagley with the idea of the qualities that make an ideal teacher, he received from another a practical training in the concept of scientific method and the importance of facts as a sound basis for theory. Perry G. Holden was in charge of the students when, according to the law, they were required to spend two and a half hours a day, except on Saturdays and Sundays and the long vacation which came in winter, on labor on the farm. Holden substituted investigations through projects and experiments. It was probably through Holden that Bagley acquired an abiding interest in farming, the only hobby, as he was to say quizzically, in which he indulged. This early training in scientific method was to be extended later when Bagley entered on his graduate studies. But he seems at this early age to have been impressed by teachers who were to serve him as models which he always had in mind when he discussed the ideal teacher or good teaching, or when he insisted that education is something more than instruction. Long before it became fashionable, he recognized the importance of the teacher's personality.

When Bagley graduated in 1895 his expectation of entering a career for which the agricultural college had prepared him was doomed to disappointment. He graduated in a period of depression and the only opportunity open to him was a post in a one-teacher school in Garth, Delta County, in the Upper Peninsula of Michigan. He accepted the post, which carried a salary of $40 a month, because he needed a job and without any intention of taking up teaching as a career. To his surprise he found the work both interesting and challenging in spite of its elementary character. What was challenging in the work to one who had had a scientific training was to search for scientific principles to guide him in his work.

> As projected against my training in science at college [he wrote to a former classmate in an undated letter, presumably in 1942], the work of teaching seemed pitiably lacking in trustworthy and experimentally tested scientific principles. In short, in so far as well-established facts and laws were concerned, mankind at that time knew vastly more about the raising of pigs than about the minds of children. In some of the reading that occupied the long winter evenings, however, I learned that efforts were being made to study mind in the same way that physicists and chemists had long studied matter; in the same way that biologists more recently had so successfully studied living organisms.

Insignificant as a one-teacher school in a simple sawmill village may have been, it inspired him with an ambition to find out more about the principles of education and to inquire whether such principles could not be discovered and established by scientific methods. His work also gave him an insight into the problems that young teachers face. As he wrote in 1935:

> I recalled the heavy weather I had made for myself as a young teacher in attempting to teach reading and writing and the rudiments of arithmetic to little children, and it occurred to me that my labors, if not lightened, might at least have been enlightened if I had been thoroughly conscious of the dramatic part that these arts have played in social evolution and of the slowness with which the race learned them.[3]

The importance of race experience as a source for educational materials was to form one of Bagley's major themes throughout his career.

In order to learn something about the new science of the mind Bagley entered the University of Chicago as a graduate student in the summer quarter of 1896 and took courses in psychology and, under Jacques Loeb, in the physiology of the nervous system. Since the venture exhausted his funds and left him in debt, he returned to his school in the fall. In the following summer he borrowed money and continued his studies at the University of Wisconsin. Here in 1898 he obtained his master's degree in experimental psychology under Joseph Jastrow. He also took courses in education with M. Vincent O'Shea, who was in Bagley's opinion "the most nearly perfect gentleman" he ever met, "strikingly handsome, always immaculately groomed, with a graceful carriage and an excellent speaking voice." O'Shea's courses confirmed Bagley's opinion derived from reading the literature on the subject that the material available in education was thin. But Bagley found another model and had the satisfaction of being encouraged by O'Shea in his ambition to establish education on scientific principles.

He found the opportunity to carry his ambition further when he was so fortunate as to be appointed to a graduate fellowship at Cornell University. He was able here to study in the psychological laboratory which, under E. B. Titchener, had become the best in the country at that time, and in one of the best laboratories of neurology. Psychology and neurology should, he thought, have the same relation to education as physiology and anatomy to medicine. Titchener was a structuralist, not a functional psychologist, who was more interested in developing psychology of the mind into a science than in its applications. But if Bagley was left to himself to make the applications of psychology to education, he did learn from Titchener the meaning of scientific method and of scholarship in any field. Scholarship, he learned, involved rigor in work, keeping up with the literature in one's field, and meticulous care in drawing conclusions from incomplete data. In 1900 he obtained the Ph.D. with a dissertation on "The Apperception of the Spoken Sentence: A Study in the Psychology of Language," which was published in the *American Journal of Psychology*. After obtaining the Ph.D. he remained at Cornell University as an assistant to Titchener through the summer of 1900 and the following semester.

Bagley was one of the first of his generation to attempt to build up a science of education on the basis of psychology, neurology, and biology. He discovered later that in this he was overoptimistic and that the methods of the natural sciences could not be applied to the study of mental and social phenomena as simply as they were applied to physical and biological phenomena. In 1914 he was to write, "Twenty years ago, when I began the study of education, I was convinced that the problems could be adequately described, formulated, and solved in terms of nerve cells and nerve fibers. These concepts of physiological psychology had their brief day and added their small mite to educational theory."[4] Nevertheless, these studies had a profound effect upon him and furnished the basis for his first book, *The Educative Process*, which marked a distinct departure from the traditional approach to the study of education.

In February 1901, Bagley became the principal of an elementary school in St. Louis where, under the supervision of practitioners like F. Louis Soldan and Ben Blewett, he received the discipline that he needed. While he learned the details of his job from his supervisors, the more lasting impression on him was left by the influence of William Torrey Harris on the development of the school system of St. Louis. It was not the Hegelian philosophy which Harris espoused that impressed him, for he admitted that he did not understand it. It was rather "the dynamic value of a richly conceived and rigidly wrought system of fundamental principles" that he carried away from St. Louis.[5] It was here that his own educational theories began to take shape under the necessity of applying what he regarded as "scientific" principles to the imperative need of getting results.[6]

Owing to the illness of his wife, Florence MacLean Winger, he was compelled to seek a better climate for her and left St. Louis in 1902. She had been a fellow student at Cornell University, and they had married in August 1901. Bagley was to express in many of his books his indebtedness to her for encouragement, sympathetic inspiration, and helpfulness as a trained psychologist. She was a woman of strong character and positive views, who undoubtedly exercised a strong influence on her husband while remaining in the background.

In this search for a better climate Bagley accepted an appointment at the State Normal College at Dillon, Montana, and also served as director of the training school. It was here that he was successful in overcoming local objections to using the public school as a training school and its pupils as "guinea pigs." His success was to be marked much later when the school was named the "Bagley School." He taught psychology as related to education, biology, and education, and modernized the training school. From 1903 to 1906 he also served as superintendent of the Dillon public schools, and in 1904 became vice-president of the College. In the midst of all these activities he found time to write the book which he had planned for some years, *The Educative Process.* The book was a pioneer in many ways and contained a reference to one of the early experiments on transfer of training, conducted by one of his colleagues, Dr. Carrie B. Squires. He made still another contribution as one of the founders and editors of *Intermountain Education,* the first school journal in the Northern Rocky Mountain region.

In 1906 Bagley resigned from his positions in Dillon to become superintendent of the training school and instructor in educational theory in the State Normal School at Oswego, New York. Here he wrote his second book, *Classroom Management,* which was published in 1907 and did not go out of print until 1946. The summer of 1907 he spent in studying schools in European countries. By this time his two books had won for him a reputation which brought offers of three university professorships in 1908.

Of the three positions offered to him Bagley accepted an appointment as professor of education at the University of Illinois. In 1909 he became director of the University's School of Education and of the summer session. In the nine years that he remained at the University of Illinois he was able to develop the School of Education into one of the leading institutions of its kind in the Middle West. He was generously supported by the administration and enjoyed the sympathetic interest of members of other departments in the University than his own. Among these were Steven S. Colvin, a psychologist, and Boyd H. Bode, a philosopher. With Colvin, Bagley collaborated in the preparation of *Human Behavior: A First Book in Psychology for Teachers* (1913), which went through several editions and was re-edited in 1929 after Colvin's death by Bagley with the cooperation of Marion E. Macdonald. With Bode, Bagley enjoyed a lifelong friendship, which continued with friendly controversies after Bode left the University of Illinois to become professor of the philosophy of education at the Ohio State University and to espouse the pragmatist view of education of which Bagley was the outstanding critic.

The School of Education had a distinguished faculty to which Bagley added others who were to make their reputations in the field of education. The faculty included in the history of education Lewis F. Anderson; in secondary education Charles Hughes Johnston; in the field of mental tests and measurements Guy M. Whipple; and in elementary education Lotus D. Coffman, who was later to become dean of the College of Education and then president of the University of Minnesota. To this group Bagley at one time hoped to add John Dewey but his hope was doomed to disappointment. The School of Education flourished, gained prestige, and attracted graduate students, some of whom were to assume leadership in other educational institutions. In 1914 the first two degrees of Doctor of Philosophy, with education as a major, were granted by the University.

Bagley did not limit his activities to the directorship of the School of Education. He combined the class work of his professorship and the supervision of both graduate and undergraduate students with the necessary task in a state institution of promoting public relations. He began to be in demand as a lecturer, and in 1913 he participated in the first of his many surveys — that of the public schools of Leavenworth, Kansas. He also managed to find time to prepare (in addition to his collaboration with Colvin on *Human Behavior*) three books: *Crafts-*

manship in Education, which consisted of lectures that he had delivered (1911); *Educational Values* (1911); and *School Discipline* (1915). In 1911–12 he was president of the National Society for the Study of Education. A year earlier he had been one of the four founders of the *Journal of Educational Psychology* and served as one of its four editors until 1917. He was also editor of *School and Home Education* from 1912 to 1921.

Throughout this period his interest in improving the professional preparation of teachers and in raising the status of the profession was constantly growing. He recognized early that one of the chief weaknesses of American education was the number of immature, untrained teachers and the brief tenure in their positions. To this he constantly directed attention until the time came for him to expound the principles that he had in mind for the improvement of teacher preparation. But before that opportunity arrived he became one of the leading proponents for the establishment of a professional honor society. It was at the University of Illinois that this society, Kappa Delta Pi, was established in 1911. The chief purpose of the society was to promote the standards of scholarship and research in institutions for the preparation of teachers and to confer the honor of membership on those students who gave evidence of ability, character, scholarship, and professional promise. Later the Laureate Chapter of the society was established for more mature men and women who had already attained a reputation in the field of educational scholarship. No distinctions were made between the different levels of professional service. This, indeed, was to be expected from a man like Bagley who preferred to be addressed as "Mister" rather than "Doctor" or "Professor," who always referred to himself as a "teacher" and not as a university professor, and, finally, who remarked on several occasions that "there are no humble positions in the educational service." Nor was it intended that distinctions of sex, color, creed, or race should enter into the selection of members.

Bagley's interest in Kappa Delta Pi was more than academic. He played an active part in its development and activities as a member, as an officer, as a Laureate member, and as counselor.

His influence on raising standards went far beyond his influence on the society's progress. At the end of the first twenty-five years of the existence of the society, the historian of this period was able to write:

> In the midst of innumerable duties pertaining to his professional duties, he gave generous support to actions influencing the Society's growth. Without the close association of his name with that of Kappa Delta Pi it would have been extremely difficult, if not impossible, for other officers to succeed in the Council's united efforts to further the welfare of the young Society. Dr. Bagley's championing of the teachers colleges led to widespread expansion of chapters among these institutions. Without his endorsement and zeal the Laureate Chapter probably could not have been established.[7]

In his report at Convocation, 1936, the Executive President of the Society stated: "Your Laureate Counselor, Dr. William C. Bagley, has been largely instrumental in making the Society what it is to-day. His willingness to give counsel and the wisdom of his suggestions have made him a most valuable member of the Executive Council through many years."[8]

Bagley's association with the society continued until his death in 1946. Because it throws so much light on him as a man and summarizes so well the ideals for which he stood and which will stand out repeatedly as his educational theory is unfolded in later chapters, the following quotation from *An Appreciation* by the Society's Executive Council on the occasion of his death is pertinent:

> The Council could rely on his human interests for guidance when questions of cultural or interracial import arose. As a cultivated man he was always an inspiration. His genial manner and gracious personality won for him an immediate place in the hearts of all members of Kappa Delta Pi, students and faculty alike. His sympathetic counsel, sparkling wit and inimitable little chuckle will be missed. . . . As a modest unassuming person he believed in the simple virtues. He felt that their realization, achieved in human beings through education in the broadest sense, would advance civilization. . . . As a friend of teacher education he strove without ceasing to raise the level of the teaching profession. His interest in educational standards and the welfare of both teacher and student brought to the Council energetic leadership in and support of endeavors for better teacher preparation and a higher quality of instruction.[9]

By 1911, when Kappa Delta Pi was established, Bagley was already recognized as a leader of educational thought, a constructive critic with a definite and convinced philosophy of education, and a courageous opponent of fads and "half-baked" theories. While he was sympathetic to the scientific development of education, he recognized its limitations. Only once did he venture into an investigation based on frequencies when, with Harold Rugg and members of a seminar, he made a study of *The Content of American History as Taught in the Seventh and Eighth Grades: An Analysis of Typical School Textbooks.*[10] There is no evidence that he pursued this type of investigation further; if an explanation may be hazarded, this was because an entirely different opportunity was opened to him to make a contribution of much larger scope to the improvement of American education.

By 1914 there was no doubt that Bagley was recognized as an outstanding leader in American education. He was in demand as a speaker and played a leading part in the activities of the National Education Association as well as in the educational affairs of Illinois. He was not only an able and interesting lecturer, but a keen controversialist. Always polite and courteous in controversy, he never pulled his punches and always manifested the courage of his convictions. What is striking in his addresses was the practical emphasis, for he believed that it was most important in talking to teachers to be as concrete as possible and to avoid disquisitions on theories that had not been tried and could not be demonstrated. His debate with Dr. David Snedden on the fundamental distinction between vocational and liberal education, which took place at the N.E.A. meeting in St. Paul in 1914, marked him as an opponent to be reckoned with. But it did more; it attracted the attention of Dean James E. Russell of Teachers College, Columbia University, who is reported to have said that Bagley was a man whom he would prefer to have speak in such debates as a member of the Teachers College faculty.

Bagley had established a reputation by 1914 not only in the field of educational theory and practice but also in the field of the education and status of teachers. The Carnegie Foundation for the Advancement of Teaching, interested in the improvement of professional preparation, turned its attention to an inquiry into the status of teacher training with a view to its improvement. It was decided to concentrate on conditions in Missouri, and to undertake the study under the direction of Dr. William S. Learned of the Foundation's staff. Bagley was invited to join the group that conducted the survey. Until 1917 he continued his work at the University of Illinois, giving some time to the Missouri survey. In 1917 Dean Russell invited him to join the faculty of Teachers College to organize a new department "concerned with the work of the normal schools and teachers' training classes . . . and the organization, management, and curriculum of schools for the training of teachers." He was also expected to give a course in the theory of education. He resigned his position in the School of Education of the University of Illinois as of August 31, 1917, but was granted a year's leave of absence by Teachers College to enable him to complete his work on the Missouri investigation. In the report published by the Carnegie Foundation in 1918 under the title, *The Professional Preparation of Teachers for American Public Schools,* Bagley was credited with the preparation of the section on the Curriculum. He began his work at Teachers College in 1918 and was the first in the country to offer courses on the general subject of the preparation of teachers for the public schools and of teachers and administrators for normal schools and teachers colleges. The contribution that he made to raising the standards of teacher preparation, both academically and professionally, will be discussed in a later chapter. Here it may be noted that it was due largely to the work of Bagley and his immediate colleagues that the term "training of teachers" was abandoned in favor of "preparation" or "education" of teachers.

A new field of professional activity was thus opened up for Bagley as a result of his work for the Carnegie Foundation survey and his appointment at Teachers College as a specialist on the preparation of teachers. He became the recognized authority on this subject and was invited to participate in numerous surveys with responsibility in practically all of them for the section on teaching personnel and the education of teachers. These surveys included: Baltimore (1920), Cleveland School of Education (1921–22), New York State Rural Schools (1922–23), Massachusetts Higher Education (1922–23), New Mexico State Institutions of Higher Education (1922), Louisiana (1923–24), Pennsylvania (1924–25), St. Louis Harris Teachers College (1928), New Jersey (1928), Florida (1929), and North Carolina Negro Colleges (1930–31). From 1930 to 1933 he was a member of the Board of Consultants for the National Survey of the Education of Teachers, which was conducted by his colleague, Dr. E. S. Evenden. In 1932, with Dr. Paul Monroe and Dr. Edgar W. Knight, he was a member of the Commission invited by the Government of Iraq to study the educational problems of the new kingdom and recommend plans for the development of a school system. In connection with his special interest he devoted his sabbatical year, 1925–26, to a study of elementary education and the education of teachers in France, Germany, Czechoslovakia, and England. The information he then obtained he frequently used for purposes of comparison and illustration.

In the midst of all these activities Bagley found time to serve as a member of the N.E.A. Commission on Emergency in Education (1918–21), and as editor-in-chief of *National School Service* for the Committee on Public Information (1918–19) and of the *Journal of the National Education Association.* In the same period the list of his own publications, including two books written in collaboration with others, continued to expand. In 1915 he published *School Discipline;* in 1918 he began his collaboration with Dr. Charles A. Beard in the preparation of American histories for schools; in 1920 he published, with John A. H. Keith, *The Nation and the Schools: A Study of the Application of the Principle of Federal Aid to Education in the United States;* and in 1924, with the same co-author, *An Introduction to Teaching,* the first of a new series, the American Teachers College Series.

The educational deficiencies revealed by the draft statistics during World War I, the social changes that took place after the war, and the emergence of progressive education and its concomitants provided Bagley with ample texts for critical discussion and for constructive suggestions of fundamental principles as the essential basis for a sound system of national education.

He was seriously disturbed by the revelation of the number of illiterates and of young draftees who could not speak English and were ignorant of the basic facts of the history and ideals of their country. These revelations only helped to provide additional arguments for his plea for wider cooperation in the maintenance and administration of schools than the traditional local system. They also helped to strengthen his plea for the better preparation and status of teachers. As a result he joined in the movement for Federal aid for education as a measure to eliminate the existing inequalities in the provision and maintenance of schools and to establish some kind of standards to be achieved but without control.

What aroused him most at this time, however, were the interpretation that was placed upon the results of the Army Intelligence Tests conducted during the war and the claims made for intelligence tests in general. The major question raised by Bagley was what the tests measured — native ability or the results of learning. He disputed the claim that the tests measured native endowment, and adduced factual evidence, state by state, in favor of the influence of education. He feared that the exaggerated claims made by some psychologists for the validity of intelligence tests would deprive boys and girls of their rightful opportunities and would seriously affect the preparation of the nation's citizens. He was particularly stirred when it was argued from the results of the Army Intelligence Tests not only that all whites were superior in intelligence, but that among the whites those of Nordic origin were superior to the rest. His criticisms gave rise to serious debates and controversies, but the net results were in Bagley's favor and arguments for the absolutist value of the IQ gradually died down after the publication of a series of papers, bearing directly or indirectly on the subject, in his book, *Determinism in Education* (1925). However, even though his arguments were clear as crystal, there were still some who charged Bagley with opposing measurements in education, a charge for which there was no foundation whatever.

This was not the only occasion on which his work was misinterpreted. When his book, *Education, Crime, and Social Progress,* was published in 1931, there were not lacking critics who charged that Bagley held crime to be the result of education. And yet the first sentence of his Preface should have protected him against such a charge. Here he wrote:

> It is very far from the writer's purpose in the following pages to suggest that education has been a causative factor in bringing about conditions so unsavory as those reflected in our very heavy crime ratios, our high and still-mounting divorce rates, and the wide prevalence of corruption in public office.[11]

No one familiar with Bagley's contributions to educational thought from his earliest publication on could have been ignorant of the emphasis that he placed on education and conduct and on the development of attitudes and ideals, or on education as an instrument of society to promote stability and progress. Equally from the earliest years of his career he regarded it as his mission to expose the weaknesses in American education with a view to replacing them with elements of strength. In an article on "School Management," which he wrote in 1911 for Monroe's *Cyclopedia of Education* (Volume V, pages 274 ff.), he pointed out that "certain conditions that now prevail in America combine with certain social causes to make the problem of school discipline unusually acute." His study from that time on took the form of social analysis to discover the nation's needs and methods for invigorating education as an instrument of social progress.

Viewed from this standpoint *Education, Crime, and Social Progress* stemmed in essence from the same principles as those which inspired Bagley to become the outstanding critic of progressive education. When analyzed in the light of criticisms by the accepted leaders of the movement, John Dewey and Boyd H. Bode, many points of correspondence can be found between them and Bagley's constant criticisms. He found progressive education lacking in a comprehensible social aim, and overemphasizing the individual, his needs, and his immediate desires. He could see nothing but chaos and confusion in the progressive attitude to the curriculum, and he was skeptical about any method that was proclaimed as the "only" method that a teacher could employ successfully. Above all he feared the effects on society of what he regarded as an element of weakness rather than of strength. When the Essentialist Committee was formed in 1938, the tide had already begun to set against progressive education which dwindled under the continued criticism of an aroused public. It should not be forgotten, however, that, despite his constant criticisms, Bagley was always ready to acknowledge the "increments" to American education from what was sound in progressive education.

Before the time for his retirement from active work at Teachers College, Columbia University, he contributed three more books to the country's educational literature. In 1934 he published *Education and Emergent Man: A Theory of Education with Particular Application to Public Education in the United States.* In this volume Dr. Bagley came nearer to presenting a comprehensive account of his philosophy of education as applied to the major problems with which it is concerned than in any of his other works.

In 1936 he delivered the annual Kappa Delta Pi Lecture, which was published in the following year with the title, *A Century of the Universal School.* The book is more than a historical account of the development of elementary education in a number of countries over one hundred years. It is rather a profession of the author's abiding faith in the upward expansion of mass education and its meaning for human progress. In an Editorial Introduction to the volume the editor, Dr. Alfred L. Hall-Quest, wrote:

> It was peculiarly appropriate that Dr. Bagley as co-founder of the Society should appear as the Society's lecturer on this occasion [the twenty-fifth anniversary of its establishment]. For more than a generation a courageous and critical champion of universal education as the firm foundation of national welfare, the author is noted here and abroad for his staunch support of the educational philosophy which

exalts common-school education as the agency now universally employed for transmitting to the young the rich heritage of racial culture and directing the nation's children toward a mastery of the elements of the knowledge and skills essential to civic co-operation. It was Dr. Bagley's concern for better informed and more professionally conscientious teachers that quickened his support of the founding of Kappa Delta Pi as an honor society in education with a co-educational membership and high intellectual attainments as its purpose.[12]

The third book, prepared in cooperation with Dr. Thomas Alexander, was published in 1937 under the title *The Teacher of the Social Studies,* and constituted Part XIV of the Report of the Commission on the Social Studies of the American Historical Association. The book is in two parts, of which Dr. Bagley prepared the first, "The Teacher of the Social Studies in the United States," and introduced the subject with two chapters on "The Profession of Teaching in the United States" and "The Education of Teachers in the United States," both excellent summaries of his various discussions of the subjects over a period of about twenty-five years. Of the author the Chairman and Director of the Investigation, Dr. A. C. Krey, wrote:

> The Commission was therefore peculiarly fortunate in having the help of W. C. Bagley as chairman of its committee on the teacher. Few if any scholars still alive in education had had as many years of experience in teacher training or rendered as distinguished service in this field. His publications reveal not only his interest in the technical aspects of the problem but equally his keen interest in society and the school in relation to it.[13]

In 1930 Bagley became associated with the Columbia Broadcasting System, Inc., as educational adviser in the development of the System's radio program for schools. Known first as the "American School of the Air," the name of the section with which Bagley was associated was changed to "School of the Air of the Americas," when the radio programs, translated into Spanish, began to be used in some of the Latin American countries. In 1935 CBS awarded him its bronze medal "For Distinguished Services to Radio Art," an honor previously conferred on Paul Muni, Admiral Byrd, and Charles A. Lindbergh. Bagley wrote enthusiastically in 1930 about the possibilities of radio programs not only for schools but also for adults who had little formal education but who could listen and receive some intellectual stimulus through radio. But for schools he was definitely of the opinion that broadcasts must be regarded as supplementary aids and could never take the place of face-to-face contact of teacher and learner.

> If in a measure commensurate with the time they consume [he wrote], they can incite learners to increased efforts, if they can bring into the school something that cannot be brought so effectively in other ways, both their cost to the sponsors and their use by the schools will be justified.[14]

With all the activities so far described – surveys, editing journals, lecturing, and writing articles and books – Bagley was also able to build up a department at Teachers College, Columbia University, which attracted men and women who were to become in turn leaders in the field of teacher preparation. There were few who were as interested in his students as was Bagley, and few as careful, meticulous, and dedicated to the task of helping them whether in class or in his office when they came to consult him about the work on which they were engaged or on personal matters, for he was genuinely interested in his students. And yet, although recognized as a master of his subject, he always showed evident signs of nervousness before he entered a classroom or mounted a platform. But once started, usually with a slight nervous cough, he continued not only unperturbed but ready to answer questions or to enter into a debate with courage and always with conviction. Following what he regarded as characteristics of a master teacher, he was always polite, always gentlemanly, and always ready with a quip or joke, delivered with a quiet chuckle and with a sparkle in his eyes. His voice was well controlled, for he regarded the proper use of the voice as an essential quality in a teacher. But when he wished to be emphatic he had a way of bending at the knees and then raising himself to his full height, looking directly at his audience, and making the particular point that he had in mind.

Bagley's kindness and geniality and readiness to help at all times won him the respect of his students and his colleagues.

Nothing made him happier in his last years at Teachers College than the dinners given in his honor on his birthday by his students in the College or by former students wherever he might be on that occasion. In 1939 former students, wherever he had taught, subscribed to a fund to be used, among other purposes, to have his portrait painted. The portrait painted by Howard L. Hildebrand now hangs in a room at Teachers College side by side with other notables in the history of the institution.

In 1939 Bagley reached the age of retirement and at the close of summer session of that year he left Teachers College, only to take up another job. The Carnegie Corporation of New York, wishing to recognize the great services of James McKeen Cattell to science through the medium of *Science* and to education through *School and Society,* which he had established in 1915, purchased the latter journal from him. The Corporation invited Bagley to organize a non-profit-making society to own and control the journal. He accepted this responsibility and the Society for the Advancement of Education was organized with Bagley as editor and manager. He was able to make the journal pay its own way (it had never been a source of profit) and in a little less than two years it was out of the red. The outbreak of war, however, made Bagley wonder how long it would remain in the black. It survived successfully and was still a going concern when its editor died in August 1946. *School and Society* continued in the tradition established by its founder except that its contents touched on more educational levels than in Cattell's days. In editing the journal Bagley was just as meticulous and nervous as when he used to prepare his lectures. He devoted hours to the careful study of an article submitted for publication and, wherever necessary, to discover the *mot juste.* In July 1944, the American College Publicity Association sent Bagley the following citation: "To *School and Society,* weekly educational journal, for distinguished service in the interpretation of higher education." Here, as in all his activities, he was sympathetic and objective.

To the honors received on this occasion and for his services to radio may be added the honorary degree of D.Ed. conferred on him in 1919 by Rhode Island State College, where his admired master teacher, Howard Edwards, was president; and the degree of LL.D. conferred on him by his alma mater, Michigan State College, in 1940.

Bagley was proud of the honors conferred on him but these and the leadership that he had attained in the profession never gave him a feeling of superiority, and one of his lasting personal characteristics was his modesty. Although he was proud of his honors, what filled him with greater pleasure was the realization that time proved him to be right both in the philosophical position which he maintained throughout his career and in his criticisms of educational movements which he believed were unsound and detrimental to the interests of the nation. In 1942, in an article in which he discussed "Illiteracy and Near-Illiteracy in the Selective Age Groups" and the accumulation of causes that produced these conditions, he stated that he felt that

> . . . he may be risking his job and whatever professional status he may have. He recalls that just twenty years ago he was drummed out of the camp of the psychologists because he insisted that the IQ represented something that was not wholly predetermined in the genes. It seems now that he was right at that time – and he has a suspicion that he is right in his present contentions.[15]

In 1933, when he delivered an address on a subject assigned to him, he stated in his opening remarks that he doubted whether he could add anything new on the subject, "The Task of Education in a Period of Rapid Change." "But," he went on, "I have developed in a fairly long professional life the unpleasant habit of disagreeing with most of my fellow-workers."[16] In an editorial in *Educational Method* in the same year Bagley was charged with standing resolutely in opposition to almost every innovation proposed in education.

> In 1914, Bagley opposed vocational education; in 1916, he fought the junior high school; in 1917, he took his stand for sound scholarship in teacher-training institutions; in 1920, he challenged intelligence testing; in 1924, he attacked scientific curriculum making; in 1929, he demanded moral ingraining and stormed against "kick psychologies"; since then he has continued his fight on all fronts. Truly a doughty warrior![17]

Bagley was able, in the same issue of the journal, to deny all the charges. He had drafted a bill, which was introduced in the Illinois legislature, proposing state subsidies for vocational education in secondary schools. He had not opposed intelligence testing but only the claim that what was tested was native intelligence. He had been director of the California Curriculum Study in 1924–25, but had criticized the multiplication of curricula adapted to local conditions and neglecting a common basic culture. In opposing the junior high school movement, he was critical only of the premature differentiation of the curriculum. There was only one innovation for which he had always fought – "the innovation that would put a competent and cultured teacher into every American classroom."[18]

The editorial in *Educational Method* had been stimulated by Bagley's address before the Department of Superintendence of the N.E.A. in Minneapolis (February 27, 1932) on "Modern Educational Theories and Practical Considerations."[19] The editorial stated that Bagley had "almost" willfully misrepresented progressive education. Bagley's criticisms, however, were not controverted and the address proved to be one of the most telling and effective criticisms to which progressive education had been exposed. Again Bagley showed his courage and confidence when he concluded the address with the words: "But even though my profession may persist in the pleasant pursuit of chasing butterflies, I still maintain that I would rather be right than Progressive." As he sat down, his friend and philosophical opponent, Boyd H. Bode, is reported to have whispered to him: "Don't worry, Bill; you will never be either." He never was a Progressive but time proved that he was right.

CHAPTER 2

CONTEMPORARY EDUCATIONAL DEVELOPMENTS

WILLIAM CHANDLER BAGLEY TOOK UP THE PROFESSION OF teaching at a time when both the theory and the practice of education entered on a period of transition. With the conquest of the frontier there began a period of social, economic, and political changes which inevitably exercised an important influence on the course of education. A rapid industrial development began and with it a new expansion in the areas of commerce, transportation, and communication. This expansion continued through the twentieth century with the multiplication of new sources of power and challenged the inventiveness of a people who had already displayed a genius for inventions and innovations, the spirit of which also infected the progress of educational development.

The conquest of the frontier and the development of large-scale industry were accomplished by an increase in the country's population, both by natural process and by immigration. At the same time the larger concentration of industry produced a redistribution of the population and the rapid growth of cities. The industrial economy gradually superseded the predominantly agricultural economy of the nineteenth century and in turn helped to promote the mechanization of agricultural production.

These factors would in any case have produced some changes in the character of the American people. But America came of age more rapidly, first, because of the sense of national consciousness aroused and stimulated by the Spanish-American War, and second, because of the participation of the nation in two world wars from which she emerged as a leading international power. Attention to the development of a sense of national consciousness was also directed by the increasing number of immigrants different in origin and cultural background from their predecessors in the eighteenth and nineteenth centuries; "Americanization" became an important aim in education.

Urbanization, which was inevitable in a country destined for advanced technological development, had its disadvantages. The influx of population, and particularly of immigrants who sought the comfort and aid of their fellow-nationals, too often produced slums. At the same time there was a tendency to exploit the immigrants industrially. Both factors stimulated a certain social consciousness and humanitarianism which sought to improve the lot of those who could not defend themselves and to curb the trends to exploitation and monopolies on the part of big business.

The era of prosperity, which began and continued in the twentieth century, despite depressions and recessions, induced a higher standard of living. But the charge was not infrequently made that wealth, accompanied by a declining sense of values and the disappearance of traditional moral controls, had a certain debilitating effect. The charges were allegedly substantiated by statistics of crime, the rise of juvenile delinquency, and the general decline of family life and parental control.

The changes in American life described up to this point would have demanded new adjustments and new orientations and emphases in the nation's education. The development of urbanization made possible the construction of larger and more schools whose number required more expert systems of administration than had prevailed hitherto. The improvement of means of transportation had its effect on the promotion of consolidation of schools and transportation of pupils in rural areas. Even before these social and economic changes took place, new developments had been foreshadowed, not only in the general theory of psychology but also in the psychology of childhood and of adolescence. Partly as a consequence of the study of the interests and growth of children, and, more particularly, as the result of new approaches to the philosophy of education, the nineteenth-century tradition of education, especially at the elementary stage, was challenged in all its aspects; secondary education was to be similarly affected later. The foundations for a revolutionary period in education began to be laid in the last two decades of the nineteenth century; the full effects did not actually become apparent until about 1915 and more definitely after 1919 when the Progressive Education Association was established. Long before those dates, however, there were evidences of efforts at innovations which, though not infrequent, never succeeded in establishing themselves for long in the public school systems.

In general the chief criticism of the traditional curriculum and methods was that they were static, uniform, and unchanging despite the changing conditions of society. That there was a definite and fixed conception of what to teach and how to teach the same subjects to all pupils, irrespective of differences of capacity, is no doubt true. Learning was accomplished either by repetition and memorization or through fear of the punishments that awaited failure, inattention, or bad conduct. Further, the methods were based, on the one hand, on a psychology which had a long tradition that could be traced as far back as Aristotle, and, on the other, on the belief that learning subject content that was hard or beyond the understanding of the pupils trained the mind to deal with other content and situations.

The attack on the traditional, metaphysical psychology came from two directions, both in Germany. In 1879 Wilhelm Wundt opened a laboratory for the experimental study of psychology in Leipzig and sought to place the subject on a scientific foundation. Two American students — G. Stanley Hall and J. McKeen

Cattell – introduced the ideas and methods of Wundt to the United States. Hall established a laboratory for experimental psychology at Johns Hopkins University in 1883 and, after he became president of Clark University, made that institution a center for research in various aspects of psychology. Hall had also been influenced by Wilhelm Preyer, author of *Die Seele des Kindes* (published in 1882 and translated as *The Mind of the Child* in 1890), and assisted in the development of child study and research into the nature and growth of the child. The promotion of child study was stimulated by the formation in 1888 of the Society for the Study of Child Nature, followed in 1908 by the organization of the Federation for Child Study which later became the Child Study Association of America. The child study movement helped to direct attention to the health of the child, his interests and tempo of growth and development, and particularly to his status as an individual.

J. McKeen Cattell, who established a psychological laboratory at Columbia University, was instrumental in introducing into psychological research the statistical methods already developed in England by Francis Galton and Karl Pearson. Another contributor to the movement for the scientific study of psychology (and consequently of education) was William James through his *Principles of Psychology* (1890) and *Talks on Psychology of Interest to Teachers* (delivered in 1891 but not published until later). The work of both leaders was combined in the work of their student, Edward Lee Thorndike, who, more than any other worker in the field, applied the lessons of modern psychology to the study of the development of the human being from infancy to old age. Thorndike's work covered every aspect of psychology that concerned the educative process – original nature and nurture, heredity and environment, individual differences of capacity, and the learning process. He propounded the principle of Stimulus–Response, or S–R bonds, as the basis of learning which held sway for several decades until Thorndike himself criticized the misinterpretations to which this principle had been subjected. For a time its acceptance exercised an influence on curriculum making and led to an emphasis on "specificity" and the enumeration of the frequency of facts as a measure of their value for learning.

Thorndike, through his research, helped with others to undermine the traditional belief in the doctrine of formal discipline and transfer. Following the lead of William James in this country, Thorndike was a leader in the general attack on faculty psychology which had prevailed in the nineteenth century. Of more permanent importance was Thorndike's application of statistical methods to the measurement of intelligence, which helped to reinforce his work on individual differences of ability and made possible the development and use of tests to measure achievement in the various aspects of school work and intellectual activity in general. Through his publications and his work at Teachers College, Columbia University, he introduced a new note into the psychology of education. A similar influence was exercised in other centers for the study of education – at the University of Chicago by Charles H. Judd, and at Stanford University by Lewis M. Terman. Many of the reforms which took place in education in the second decade of the present century can be traced back to a better understanding of child growth and development, of the learning process, and of individual differences. There were some, in fact, who claimed that the so-called "science of education" could give a more complete and reliable guide for the conduct of the educative process than any philosophical disquisitions on the subject.

That this claim was exaggerated can be verified by a study of the philosophies of education which influenced the progress of education from the last years of the nineteenth century into the twentieth. The two most influential philosophies of this period – Herbartianism and pragmatism or instrumentalism – were founded on a psychological basis. Philosophy and psychology were inevitably linked together as correlatives in any reform movement. Both were necessarily associated in efforts to improve the curriculum and methods of instruction. Nevertheless, while the application of scientific methods to psychology produced a certain amount of reliability and certainty, there prevailed a conflict of philosophies of education. This was evidenced by the fact that school programs were in a state of flux and by an absence of agreement on their functions. The stress on change, adjustment, and reforms of different kinds has been as marked in American education as in other aspects of American life. What has been referred to as "a spread of objectives or diffusion of teaching effort" has been a characteristic of American education since the beginning of the century and is not a phenomenon which has disturbed the American public only since World War II. This characteristic is due in part to the confusion of change with progress, and in part to the emphasis placed by administrators of education on the importance of "selling" education to the public, a practice which, as in industry and commerce, invites an emphasis on innovations.

The movements for the reform of American education from the points of view of both psychology and philosophy may be said to have begun about 1890. There had been reforms before that date – the development of object lessons at Oswego, New York, by Edward A. Sheldon, and the Hegelian reforms in St. Louis by William Torrey Harris. The reform which, for about a quarter of a century, had the widest influence was also of foreign origin but was gradually better adapted to the American situation. A purely American philosophy of education began to be elaborated by John Dewey in the last years of the nineteenth century but did not become dominant until the publication of his *Democracy and Education* in 1916.

The first of the two reform philosophies was that of Johann Friedrich Herbart, which was brought back to the United States by American educators who had studied in Leipzig or Jena under exponents of Herbart's theory. Among these followers of Herbartianism were Charles DeGarmo, C. C. Van Lieuw, and Charles A. and Frank M. McMurry, who directed their attention particularly to the improvement of methods of instruction and subsequently to the more careful selection of the content of the curriculum. The basis of their reforms was to stimulate and develop the interest of the pupils, to associate all learning with what had already been learned, and to train the pupils to reach generalizations or conclusions from what they learned. Their efforts were directed to "psychologizing" the educative process along the lines of the "five formal steps" developed out of Herbart's philosophy. If they did not introduce radical reforms in the curriculum of the elementary schools, the Herbartians did succeed in emphasizing that instruction must proceed with and elicit the interest, understanding, and intellectual activity of the pupils. While a scientific attack was being made on various educational problems, the Herbartians directed attention to teaching as an art and some were outstanding themselves as master teachers. Although they did not revolutionize the curriculum or its content, they introduced methods of approach, like type studies, topical lessons, concentration and correlation, anticipating later practices which were regarded as innovations such as the project method, unit lessons, and the core and broad-fields organization of the curriculum. The Herbartians differed from the theorists who displaced them later by adhering to a traditional curriculum, trimmed of nonessentials with little appeal to the interest of the pupils, while their successors sacrificed a stable curriculum of subjects in favor of the pupils' own interests and felt needs, which were assumed to emerge spontaneously. A new vitality was injected into elementary education, and a break began to be made from the traditional American practice of learning by rote and memorization, or the recitation method. This method may have been useful when teachers were untrained and not too well educated, but it had no place in a system in which the teacher was to assume a new position as one who is to help pupils to educate themselves. The function of the teacher was not understood to be that of hearing pupils recite but of teaching pupils how to study.

The Herbartian method failed chiefly because of the too literal acceptance of the "five formal steps," which were too rigidly adhered to and resulted in stilted formalism and monotony. But there was another movement which led to the decline of Herbartianism, and that was the application of scientific methods to the process of education. The chief contributions of the Herbartians had been to methods of instruction; the new interest stimulated by the science of education was directed to the discovery of an answer to a question raised earlier by Herbert Spencer — "What knowledge is of most worth?" Efforts were made to find an answer in terms of the knowledge, facts, and information that pupils were likely to come across in their daily needs or in their reading, or that was socially most worth while. The method that was used took the form of job analysis or frequency counts of the activities of adult life or of the major activities of group life. The search for minimum essentials in education was sponsored by the National Education Association which in 1911 appointed the Committee on the Economy of Time. A period of curriculum reconstruction was initiated and a new specialist — the curriculum expert — soon emerged. Subject matter continued to be retained but its selection and organization of content were based on the needs of adult life and adapted to the intelligence of the pupils at their stage of maturity. A new trend had already set in which was more experimental and revolutionary, and based on a philosophy assumed to be more natively American.

The new philosophy represented a complete break with the traditional philosophies and accordingly stood as a challenge to the philosophies of education which had dominated American education. It had, however, one aspect that was rooted in the history of the country — an intense faith in education. It went beyond that faith, which sought to provide both a stabilizing influence and a preparation for citizenship, in its belief that social reconstruction could be promoted through education. That a new approach to education was foreshadowed was indicated by John Dewey's attack on the Herbartian concept of interest as something extrinsic to the real interests and needs of the child. At the same time that Dewey delivered his attack on the Herbartian concept of interest, he began to apply to education the knowledge that had been developed through the study of the child. In his own laboratory school in Chicago (started in 1896), he sought "to train children in cooperation and mutually useful living." Through his writings he directed the emphasis in education to the child with an individuality, interests, and needs of his own. To "interest" the child in subjects as such and as practiced by the Herbartians was, according to Dewey, sugar-coating something that did not in actuality represent the child's "intrinsic" or spontaneous interest which grew out of his own immediate need for expression. The Herbartians were influenced by Dewey's criticism of the doctrine of interest to the extent of dropping the name of Herbart from the title of their society, the National Herbart Society for the Scientific Study of Education, and of dedicating the Society to "the serious, continuous, and intensive study of educational problems" without any restrictive labels of dogma or doctrine other than scientific.

As already indicated, the Herbartians continued to play an important part in the progress of education and incorporated into their work whatever proved to be useful from the scientific development. Dewey's influence was marked only in the creation or reorganization of private experimental schools, mainly at the elementary level. It was some time before the fuller implications of pragmatism (or, as Dewey preferred to call his philosophy, experimentalism or instrumentalism) were fully understood. In a period when the concept of what should be taught both in elementary and secondary schools was fairly constant, the theory was enunciated that education is life and not a preparation for life, that life itself is a continuing process of adjustment to changing conditions, and that truth is not something fixed and established permanently, but a hypothesis to be tried out to see how it works. Truth can only be known by its consequences, and the test is whether the consequences succeed in solving the difficulties or obstacles encountered by an individual who has a purpose to carry out. Purposeful activity is accordingly important, because it stimulates the individual to think through his problems in order to find solutions. Since the end of education is growth, the method of growth is through activity rather than passive learning of extrinsic matter, even when made interesting. Not only does the spirit of activity encourage experimentation, but it is the only method by which knowledge, facts, and information, relevant to one's purpose, are acquired.

Only in this way does knowledge become an instrument for use as contrasted with passive learning which meant the acquisition of knowledge for some future use which might never arise.

The pragmatic concept of truth also applied to values. To assume the existence of values is to believe in abstractions and to teach them as such is to indoctrinate the child by authoritarian methods. The child should be put into a situation where he will develop his own values and learn by his own experiences. The business of education is to assist the child through his own experiences to develop the right attitudes and to acquire the ability to meet new situations as they arise. Only in this way, it was claimed, can growth be measured – not by the amount of knowledge, facts, and information that has been acquired. It was for this reason that educators of the pragmatic school tended to be skeptical of the use of achievement tests.

Two important points were inherent in this philosophy. The first was that the past, with its traditional truths and values to be imposed, is valuable only as it can be drawn upon for present use. This was, indeed, the point most stressed by some of Dewey's followers whose strongest arguments for the new philosophy were based on an exposition of the iniquitous practices to be found both in traditional cultures and in the tradition of education. Usually the worst in the latter tradition was compared with the best in the new. The evils of passive learning were contrasted with the creativity and self-expression that were stimulated by the methods of activity. The chief concession that was made to traditional values was to claim that the knowledge, facts, and information acquired through passive learning were acquired "incidentally" when activities were engaged in.

The second point emphasized in the pragmatic philosophy was that it got rid of traditional dualisms: school and society, the child and the curriculum, interest and effort, thought and action, learning and doing. In the main the dualisms were expected to disappear when the principle was accepted that education is life and not a preparation for life. Knowledge must not be learned and stored away for future use; it is acquired for immediate use when life is regarded as an ongoing process and when the knowledge so acquired through experience is employed to control situations. The curriculum is not fixed in advance but is something that emerges in response to the child's felt needs and purposes. And since it responds to his effort to learn it does not have to be induced by external pressures of rewards or punishments, but is a natural corollary of his interest. In the same way, because he is engaged in carrying out purposes which have meaning for him, the child learns to control himself and the issue of external discipline does not arise. Nor is there the traditional dualism of school on one side and society on the other, since the school is a society in miniature. The child develops social responsibility by sharing and cooperating in experiences with others.

Education, then, is a process of self-development through active response to "felt needs" and the effort of solving one's problems and difficulties. Hence growth, which results from the personal activity of reconstructing one's experiences, cannot be promoted by imposing or assigning subject matter to be learned. The function of the teacher is to "contrive" situations and to stand by to advise if called upon. Indeed, the word curriculum was abandoned by some devotees for "learning situations," "experiences," "arithmetic situations," and so on. Whether such trends were warranted by Dewey's writings may be judged from the following passages cited from them. In *My Pedagogical Creed* (1897) he wrote that "subject matter of the school curriculum should mark a gradual differentiation out of the primitive unconscious unity of social life." In 1916 he wrote in *Democracy and Education,* "Moreover the curriculum must be planned with reference to placing essentials first, and refinements second. The things which are socially most fundamental, that is, which have to do with the experiences in which the widest groups share, are the essentials." (The use of the word "essentials" should be noted.) In *Experience and Education* (1938) appeared the statement that the logical organization of facts and ideas must be regarded as an ideal in the educative process. Professor Boyd H. Bode, in his *Progressive Education at the Crossroads* (1938), maintained that traditional subjects had an educational value that could not be neglected without peril.

But these two leaders of the movement had already become critical of the manifestations of their philosophy in school practice where "mere knowledge" was regarded with contempt and the subject-matter organization of the curriculum was considered entirely out of date. In an article in *The New Republic* (1930) Bode wrote:

> To the casual observer American education is a confusing and not altogether edifying spectacle. It is productive of endless fads and panaceas; it is pretentiously scientific and at the same time pathetically conventional; it is scornful of the past, yet painfully inarticulate when it speaks of the future. The tremendous activity now going on in education is evidence of far-reaching social changes, but we do not seem to know what these changes signify or how they can be directed.

In the same journal Dewey stated that, although there was a great variety of experiments as reactions against traditional educational practices, there was no genuine sense of direction except an exaggerated and unfounded concept of freedom without a sense of social responsibility. To those who emphasized change as dynamic and tended to regard stability or any kind of tradition as static Dewey was able to say in his address at the Harvard Tercentenary Conference on Arts and Sciences that order and authority are the bases of stability and that freedom is needed to make change possible; there is "an intimate and organic union of the two things: of authority and freedom, of stability and change."

By the time Dewey and Bode criticized the results that came from the misinterpretations of the pragmatic philosophy of education, the child-centered school sponsored by the Progressive Education Association, founded in 1919, had almost run its course. But as Bode pointed out, the educational situation was confusing, and Dewey referred to the absence of a genuine sense of direction. The common bonds seem to have been an emphasis on the child with his freedom and his felt needs and purposes, and a scorn for traditional practices in curriculum and methods of instruction, standards, and discipline. The period, however, was not without its advantages; it introduced the idea of greater flexibility, which was emphasized despite a trend to certain conventions; it stressed the importance of the pupil's participating in his own educational development because he understood the meanings of what he was learning and doing; and it stressed the functional value of knowledge, at times with too great an emphasis on its immediacy, but sound, if broadly interpreted.

With the onset of the depression years another aspect of Dewey's philosophy began to be emphasized — the use of education for social reconstruction. Led by George S. Counts and John L. Childs the new emphasis directed attention away from the child as the center of the educative process to the community and society in general as centers from which should flow the problems and content of education. The movement culminated by the end of the 'thirties in plans for community-centered schools to promote progress in education and community living. The new trend did not gain momentum until after World War II. At that time, partly as a consequence of the revelation of educational conditions in both elementary and secondary education, and later stimulated by the challenge from Soviet Russia's launching of the round-the-orbit missile, Sputnik, a wave of criticism of the educational shortcomings arose. The defects were attributed to the vogue of progressive education in the preceding thirty years. It was unfortunate that responsibility for the development of this form of education was placed upon John Dewey whose criticisms of the interpretations of his educational philosophy in practice mounted in the 'thirties, only to be ignored.

Elementary education during the major part of the twentieth century was dominated by changes in educational theories, first with reference to methods of instruction, then to the content of education, and then to both, a trend directed to a better adjustment of the educative process to the needs and interests of the pupil. In secondary education the transformation of the high school from the traditional form with its emphasis on academic subjects was produced by changing what had been a selective type of school to a nonselective type. The Committee of Ten, reporting in 1895, and the Committee on College Entrance Requirements, whose report appeared in 1899, sought to standardize the concept of a liberal education for pupils at the secondary school level and added a few modern subjects to the traditional academic list. The reports did not represent a serious or radical revolution in secondary education.

The progress of urbanization, the development of technology, and the increasing wealth of the country encouraged an upward expansion of education – from the elementary to the high school at first and then from the high school to the two-year junior college and later, to the four-year liberal arts college. The movement represented another stage in the fulfillment of the American ideal of providing equality of educational opportunities for all the children of all the people. At least three factors contributed to bring about a gradual and radical transformation or expansion of the curricular offerings of the high schools. Of these the first was the assumed demolition of the doctrine of mental discipline on the basis of which it had for centuries been claimed that certain subjects, such as Latin and mathematics, to which foreign languages and sciences were later added, provided an intellectual training because of their difficulty for the learner. The results of several investigations of the doctrine by psychologists were interpreted to have "exploded" the doctrine. At a time when the provision of more secondary education was being urged, this interpretation strengthened the hands of the advocates who could now promise to give high school students courses and subjects suited to their needs, interests, and abilities.

These arguments of the critics of the academic tradition were further strengthened by the results of studies of eliminations and mortality in the student body. From the number of students who began to drop out of high school at the end of the first year, and the number who remained at school for four years only to fail in the final examinations, it was concluded that the curriculum was not adjusted to the abilities of the students. The door was opened still wider for the introduction of new subjects. Following the reports of the Commission on the Reorganization of Secondary Education, appointed in 1913, general agreement was reached on the *Cardinal Principles of Secondary Education* (1918) but not on what would constitute a sound secondary education. While the opportunities for education were democratized, the subjects of the secondary school were also democratized, and any subject was as good as any other subject taught for the same length of time. The only standardized requirements were the subjects approved for entrance to college, and even here, under the system of accreditation and through pressure for the acceptance of a few electives, there was a relaxation of standards. With the rapid increase in the offerings of the high school the traditional academic subjects declined in favor and receded into the background as compared with the host of other subjects that were constantly being added.

Here the third reason for the gradual transformation of the curriculum appeared. Subjects were added or fell into disfavor according as they were "functional," that is, could be applied in the life activities or occupations of the students. The traditional subjects, it was assumed, served no function either as a liberal education in modern times or for use in the ordinary routine of daily life. Further, they were difficult for the majority of the vastly increased number of students enrolled year after year. Hence, discouraged by questions like "What is the use of Latin?" or "What is the use of mathematics?" and so on, able students who might have profited from such studies refrained from taking them. Paradoxically, because such studies were traditionally associated with the concept of secondary education, students who did not have the necessary ability to pursue them successfully, nevertheless did take them.

The general result of the efforts to meet the needs of the average was a relaxation of standards and failure to provide an appropriate education for those above and those below the average. The recognition that the interests of the gifted pupils were being forgotten or ignored did not come until the fourth decade of the century, a recognition that was later forced on public attention by Soviet Russia's success in launching Sputnik. To argue in favor of the academic tradition or to direct attention to the needs of the able or gifted students was to incur the charge of advocating a special education for an intellectual elite and the creation of a cultured caste of intellectuals, which would be undemocratic. And yet the nation's needs for experts in foreign languages, mathematics, and sciences during World War II, and later to answer the challenge of Soviet Russia, served to direct attention to this problem more than ever before. The unrest in both secondary and higher education was caused not only by this challenge but was the culmination of criticisms, which had been current for some time, of the aims and content of education at this stage. For several years there had been widespread discussions of the meaning of a liberal or general education. The discussions became nationwide after the publication of the Harvard University report on *General Education in a Free Society* (1945). The issue ultimately involved not only the question of the nature of a general education but also the organization of the nation's system of education to ensure equality of opportunity for all in accordance with individual differences in ability.

Although it has always been understood that the success of a system of education depends upon the teachers, more attention was paid in the first half of the twentieth century to the provision and improvement of school buildings, to the philosophy of education, to curriculum revision, to methods of instruction, to educational psychology and tests and measurements than to the adequate preparation of teachers. Proposals looking to the improvement of the standards of admission to preparation for the profession of teaching began to be put forward in the last decade of the nineteenth century. New York State in 1890 and Massachusetts in 1894 were the first states to require the completion of a high school course for admission to the normal schools. In the rest of the country elementary school teachers were usually trained either in high schools or in normal schools which gave some secondary instruction along with the training. The supply of high schools was in fact inadequate until much later. In the main the training of elementary school teachers consisted in imparting the knowledge and skills that the teachers would require to instruct their pupils in elementary schools, plus courses in the techniques of teaching, classroom management, and induction into practice. Before 1900 there was little professional content available nor was the task of instruction considered to be more than imparting a specific and limited quantum of knowledge.

The study of education as an essential part of professional preparation was promoted at the turn of the century by Teachers College, Columbia University, and schools of education that began to be established in the universities of the country. What had been known as "pedagogy" was expanded to include the study of all the problems of education from infancy into adult life and at every level. The multiplication of high schools made it possible to raise the standards of the normal schools and to require high school graduation for admission. Some standardization was introduced with each state replacing the teaching certificates given by local authorities by certificates granted by state boards and departments of education. The effect of this practice contributed in turn to raising the standards of the normal schools. But the length of the courses in these institutions continued to be two years until about 1920, and into the two years there had to be compressed courses in academic subjects, professional studies, and teaching observation and practice.

With the changing status of elementary education, the increase in professional literature, and the broadening function of the teacher the status of the normal schools had to be changed. Elementary school teaching was no longer considered to be limited to imparting a knowledge of a fixed amount of subject matter, but was broadened to include a better understanding of each pupil as an individual, of his environment, and of his particular capacity. It was also recognized that learning did not consist of the passive absorption or memorization of lessons, but that intellectual activity on the part of the pupils must be encouraged.

Accordingly the standards of the normal schools were raised and the preparation for elementary school teachers was gradually raised from two to three, and four years in different parts of the country. The change was further marked by a change of title when normal schools began to be denominated "teachers colleges." Simultaneously the standards for certification were changed.

The volume of criticism of teacher preparation and certification was not reduced, however, despite these changes. The criticisms took various forms. It was charged that the standards of admission continued to be low, and that institutions for the preparation of teachers did not attract the able high school graduates. The chief objection was concerned with the curriculum of the teachers colleges and normal schools. The opinion was widespread that too much time was devoted to so-called professional subjects and methods of instruction and too little to academic subjects and the development of an adequate mastery of subject matter. Similar criticisms were leveled against the overemphasis on professional subjects in the certification of both elementary and secondary school teachers. Efforts to adjust the organization of academic and professional subjects to meet the needs of the schools were in general ignored not only by the critics but also by many among those responsible for the preparation of teachers. Nor was the situation changed markedly when the terminology was altered and the "training" of teachers became the "preparation" and later the "education" of teachers.

The developments in education described summarily in this chapter present the scene within which anyone destined to become a leader in the advancement of American education had to play his part as did the subject of this biography. In his earliest writings and lectures Dr. Bagley was critical of the number and frequency of innovations proposed without adequate proof of their validity or soundness. He deplored the gradual trend away from direct emphasis on social objectives for American education. He was opposed to the overemphasis on "scientific" methods in education and instruction to the neglect of the broader approach that he believed to be essential. His opposition to the curriculum revision movement was aroused by the tendency to ignore the need and importance of common elements in the educational system of a nation, particularly of a nation marked by a high degree of mobility in its population. He was always convinced that no system of education could be better than its teachers, to whose education and professional preparation he devoted so much thought. And it was out of a thorough realization of the teacher's work in the classroom that his philosophy of education grew.

CHAPTER 3

BAGLEY'S FAITH IN EDUCATION AND DEMOCRACY

THERE ARE FEW IN THIS COUNTRY WHO HAVE MANIFESTED such unbounded faith and on all occasions expressed their pride in American education with such sincere conviction as did Dr. Bagley. He never viewed the educational situation, however, with the uncritical complacency shown by some of his professional colleagues, nor was he as ready as so many of his contemporaries in the profession to abandon the best in the tradition of education and to discard what time had proved to be educationally valuable, whether in the United States or elsewhere, for the sake of what he called "the new and the bizarre" or for the plaudits of the multitude. He was, indeed, "truly a doughty warrior" in a real sense and not in the sense implied by the editor of *Educational Method* in his attack on Bagley (see page 22). He was ready to fight for what he believed to be an education that would advance the welfare and progress of the American people. In this he was not animated by the prospect of aggrandizing his professional reputation or of magnifying his own status. He realized, in fact, that in every fight that he undertook he was risking both professional status and reputation. In an article written toward the end of his career, in which he referred to his criticisms after World War I of the misuse of the results of intelligence tests and the misinterpretation of the IQ, and discussed the weaknesses manifested during World War II in mathematics and physical sciences, he wrote of himself: "It seems now that he was right at that time and he has a suspicion that he is right in his present contentions." He was not destined to live long enough to discover that he was justified by public opinion in all his criticisms and that his criticisms became common property in the years following World War II.

When he thought that a situation called for it, he never refrained from criticism, open, frank, and direct. Moreover, his criticisms were always accompanied by suggestions for correction and improvement. He was particularly interested in several distinct areas of education. He recognized the importance of a sound education for national security and stability and for the welfare and progress of the American people as much in a spiritual as in a material sense. He believed profoundly in the provision of genuine equality of educational opportunity. He was impressed with the paramount urgency of establishing a profession of teaching, respected for its professional preparation and breadth of scholarship and accorded a status commensurate with the national importance of education. Above all he valued the upward expansion of education as a means for raising the level of mass intelligence and for understanding the problems that "the common man" must meet as the citizen of a democracy. It was for these reasons that he fought so strenuously against the attempt to use the newly developed intelligence tests as instruments to deny the educability of boys and girls whose IQ did not reach a certain standard. He did more than attack; he proved conclusively that the intelligence tests did not measure native ability or endowment alone but also the influence of environment and schooling on the intelligence of the individual tested. He saw in this movement the danger of encouraging either social stratification or an aristocracy of intellectuals, both of which would, in his opinion, be detrimental to democracy.

Another contribution made by Bagley was his continued criticism of fads and innovations in education and subsequently of progressive education. He defined his own position early in his career, when he addressed the St. Louis Society of Pedagogy in 1910 and in the course of his address said:

> As I have suggested, there are always two dangers that must be avoided: the danger, in the first place, of thinking of the old as essentially bad; and, on the other hand, the danger of thinking of the new and strange and unknown as essentially bad; the danger of confusing a sound conservatism with a blind worship of established custom; and the danger of confusing a sound radicalism with the blind worship of the new and the bizarre.[1]

A few years later he said in an address before the National Education Association: "We are hearing so often to-day that the traditional methods and processes of teaching have been utterly futile that we are coming to take the statement as a fact without asking for the evidence."[2] That he retained a balanced view was indicated in a statement made in 1921: "Personally I have large sympathy with the idea of freedom from the enthrallment of purposes handed down by tradition or imposed by authority. I am quite clear that an important line of progress is in the direction of such freedom."[3]

Because he was convinced from the start of his career that in education it is important to have a sense of direction and that such a sense could be found in a sound conservatism and the lessons that could be derived from a study of race experience, Bagley was resolutely set against fads and innovations. He directed his efforts to pointing out the dangers of the radicalism, which such innovators represented, as early as 1907 and continued them persistently to the close of his career. It is when viewed in the light of his constant warnings against innovations that his criticisms of progressive education can be more readily understood. But here, as in all his critical discussions, he had positive goals and practical ideas to offer (these will be fully discussed in a later chapter). If his discussions of fads and innovations are here cited at some length, they can be justified because they are not irrelevant to an understanding of some of the causes of weakness in the American system of education, which began to be generally recognized after World War II.

In a complex process, like education [Bagley wrote in 1907], it is always necessary to keep a clear perspective. . . . But lack of perspective may easily cause some serious misplacements of emphasis, if not more disastrous consequences, under exceptional conditions. The waves of fads and reforms that sweep through the educational system at periodic intervals will have but little detrimental influence upon the teacher whose theoretical foundations are firm and stable; but the teacher who lacks secure moorings is tossed from wave to counter wave, until he either loses his bearings entirely or collapses from *mal de mer*.[4]

A few pages later he described in greater detail the nature of many proposed innovations.

In education, the evils of perverted system are the chief cause of the violent reactions which periodically affect the school system. Such standing in the educational world. These reformers would cut the reactions are often initiated by men of wide experience and high red tape of school organization; discard, once and for all, the repressive forces that confine and limit the child's activities; and leave teacher and pupil to work out each his own salvation in the chaos of confusion and disorder. These frequent and extreme reactions are often beneficial in that they call attention to useless and wasteful routine, and thus serve to stimulate a healthful reform. . . . But to discard system and organization entirely is to repudiate the basic law of all advancement; evolution is simply a progressive development toward forms that are more and more elaborately organized, and in which system and coherence take the place of chaos and incoherence.[5]

Four years later and several years before progressive education became what Bagley was to call "the dominant American theory of education," he again subjected the vagaries of reformers to close inspection. In 1911 he wrote:

It is difficult not to be depressed by the irrational radicalism of contemporary educational theory. It would seem that the workers in the higher ranges of educational activity should, of all men, preserve a balanced judgment and a sane outlook, and yet there is probably no other human calling that presents the strange phenomenon of men who are called experts throwing overboard everything that the past has sanctioned, and embarking without chart or compass upon any new venture that happens to catch popular fancy. The nonprofessional character of education is nowhere more painfully apparent than in the expression of this tendency. The literature of teaching that is written directly out of experience — out of actual adjustment to the teaching situation — is almost laughed out of court in some educational circles. But if one wishes to win the applause of the multitude one may do it easily enough by proclaiming some new and untried plan. At our educational gatherings you notice above everything else a straining for spectacular and bizarre effects. It is the novel that catches attention; and it sometimes seems to me that those who know the least about the educational situation in the way of direct contact often receive the largest share of attention and have the largest influence.[6]

This passage is noteworthy not only for its criticism of radicalism in educational theory but also for its suggestion of Bagley's own philosophy. He referred elsewhere to the constant straining for effect, to the continual state of turmoil and confusion created by the annual crop of fads and fancies, and to the rage for the new and the untried, which was in his opinion, "the rock upon which real educational progress is most likely to be wrecked."[7]

That the situation had not changed so far as innovations were concerned is indicated by a statement made by Bagley two decades later, when he discussed progressive education and "another element of weakness in American education — the tendency of the members of our profession to follow fashions with a maximum of zeal and a minimum of discrimination." This tendency, he thought, was not so much the fault of the teachers themselves but of the administrators and the public who wanted the latest.[8] Acceptance of prevailing modes and fashions, of

slogans and shibboleths which are all too often only half truths and sometimes deceptive and perilous fallacies . . . keeps the work of education in our country in a continual state of unstable equilibrium, with confused aims, congested and inarticulate programs, and necessarily superficial results.[9]

He returned to this topic again in a definitive statement of his educational theory, published in 1934.

There is no country in the world that has witnessed so many educational "reforms" during the past generation as has the United States. It has been one nostrum or cure-all after another. We have tried to improve the educational system by shuffling school grades into new divisions with new names; by adopting, one after another, different "methods" of teaching; by trying this and then that and then another pattern of organizing curricular materials. Until recently, however, we have been obtuse to the fundamental factor, more important than all others put together — namely, the teacher.[10]

There was one innovation which Bagley claimed that he had proposed and for which he had "fought in season and out of season, namely, the innovation that would put a competent and cultured teacher into every American classroom." This innovation would, he felt, do more for the advancement of American education than all other innovations together:

And I venture to suggest that, if some of my good friends had directed more time and energy toward the realization of this ideal and less to shuffling school grades into subdivisions with new names, and to constructing and reconstructing curriculum, and to ridiculing the exact and exacting and glorifying the inexact and appealing, and to other activities of the genus Hocus-pocus, we should be better off educationally, financially, and in several other ways than we are today.[11]

Many of the weaknesses and defects of American education Bagley attributed to the rapid succession of fads, innovations, and so-called reforms, put forward frequently without the benefit of being tried out in the classroom, or, if already the results of experimentation, destined to be put out of court by later experiments. He warned against the danger of attempting to construct an educational system on the quicksands of what he called "half-baked reforms" instead of on the solid rock of experience. When suggested innovations were supported by the evidences of classroom experimentation or when they could be justified in the light of social changes, he was willing to accept them. But he was never willing to sacrifice everything that man had tried out and found valuable in the long history of his cultural evolution just for the sake of keeping up with the Joneses of education. In 1910 he delivered an address, entitled "A Plea for the Definite in Education," in the course of which he said: "The best way in this world to be definite is to know our goal and then strive to attain it. In the lack of definite standards based upon the lessons of the past, our dominant national ideals shift with every shifting wind of public sentiment and demand."[12] A paper read at the meeting of the N.E.A. in 1917 bore the significant title "Are the Older School Virtues Obsolescent?"

Throughout his career Bagley was strongly motivated by his belief in the social aim of education and in a sense of social responsibility. He became increasingly disturbed by the growing tendencies to stress individualism and self-centeredness, and to make both the starting point and the ultimate end of education. He saw in such tendencies the roots of the weaknesses of American education, both moral and intellectual. His emphasis on moral development was based on his conviction that moral ideas and ideals are social in origin and contributory to social stability, welfare, and progress. In his early writings he attached particular importance to the development of habits, ideas, and ideals, and of a sense of duty and discipline not for their own sakes but as "controls of conduct" in a social setting. He frequently took occasion in his later writings to deplore the fact that such terms as duty, discipline, and responsibility had either been discarded from the vocabulary of American education, or, if mentioned at all, were treated with ridicule in the same way as the idea of "eternal verities" became an object of derision. He regretted the decline of attention in the schools to what he called "the virile qualities" and was unwilling to accept the view that to inculcate them would adversely affect the development of initiative and originality. He believed that "what is sown in the school to-day will be reaped in the next generation."[13]

The basic principle that the function of education is not only to advance intellectual development but also to contribute to the moral and social welfare of a nation prompted Bagley to examine the causes of crime and divorce ratios and other defects in the fabric of American society. Crime, divorce, and political corruption, he found, were more prevalent in this country than in any other of comparable status, and were on the increase. His discussions of this subject were misinterpreted as attempts to place responsibility for these defects upon the schools. What he actually endeavored to find out was whether the same causes that produced these defects were also responsible for the weaknesses that were becoming apparent in the schools. This point he brought out clearly in his Kappa Delta Pi Lecture delivered in 1936:

> The relative inefficiency of the universal school in the United States and its apparently increasing ineffectiveness may well cause general concern. It should be pointed out, however, that the American school has not been a negative force. In so far as I can learn after many years' study of the problem, there is no causal relationship between the weakness of the schools and the prevalence of serious crime, the high divorce rates, and other unsavory characteristics of our civilization. The school has been affected by the same weakening forces that have permitted most Americans to remain unconcerned in the face of high crime ratios and serious political corruption; for example, the mores which protect extreme localism in the control of government and the mores which reflect an extreme individualism which has permitted grave abuses to creep into certain phases of business.[14]

The tendency to discard the standards of conduct that had been handed down by the forefathers Bagley attributed always to the prosperity enjoyed by the American people in the twentieth century, which encouraged ease and comfort and gave an assurance of security. As a consequence the traditional virtues such as thrift, thoroughness, good workmanship, as well as the acceptance of a sense of duty and responsibility, were abandoned. Modern education, he felt, should be adequate to the task of instilling ideals into each generation:

> Certain it is that the present tendencies in our schools toward ease and comfort and the lines of least resistance confirm rather than counteract the operation of that *Zeitgeist* which reflects so perfectly the moral decadence that comes with prosperity — the letting loose the grip that our forefathers, who lived under sterner and harsher conditions, had upon the ideals of self-denial and self-sacrifice.[15]

He returned on a number of occasions to the thesis that material prosperity gives sanction to ease and comfort and the lines of least resistance:

> Its clear tendency is to increase the spirit of individualism — to multiply the opportunities for the gratification of individual desires, and to minimize the significance of sacrifice and renunciation. The increase of wealth and the consequent increase of leisure mean an increased moral hazard.[16]

In an article on "Education and the Two New Freedoms," published in 1943, he again made the point that the cultivation of ideals of thrift and responsibility is at basis a function of organized education. He felt that "ease, comfort, and security are inimical not only to social progress, but to the welfare and especially the mental growth of the individual."[17]

In examining the weaknesses and defects of American education in order to discover what needed to be done to create a vigorous and virile system, Bagley did not confine his attention only to the spiritual aspects. He did not miss an opportunity to point out the material causes that explained the ineffectiveness of "the universal school" which he always regarded with pride. Since he considered the teacher as "the soul and substance" of the educational situation, he deplored the low standards of preparation, the inadequacy of the normal schools for the task that they were expected to perform, and the absence of a professional spirit and consciousness. Evidences of all these deficiencies were manifested in the immaturity and short tenure of the teachers, the low salaries, and the tendency to place the emphasis on the overhead, that is, the administrative aspects which reproduced "the factory system" and gave the classroom teachers the status of "hands." It was a natural consequence of his study of these conditions that he devoted so much attention during most of his career to the preparation and status of teachers, as will appear in a subsequent chapter.

The revelations of the educational conditions throughout the nation which were brought to light by the draft requirements during World War I made a marked impression on Bagley. With the conditions of the teaching occupation he was familiar, but the draft revealed weaknesses in the American system which do not seem to have entered into his thinking before 1916. The figures of illiteracy and physical deficiencies, and the number of young persons who were not only ignorant of the English language and the ideals of American life and institutions, but had been educated, as it were, in an alien language and environment, exercised a profound influence on him and directed his attention to the country's educational needs. The training for citizenship had been proved to be inadequate. Examining the situation carefully, he concluded that one of the chief causes of the conditions that were revealed was the tradition of localism which was responsible for so much backwardness and intellectual stagnation. Combined with low standards of teacher preparation and certification and the practice of appointing local "talent" to teach in inadequate buildings and with little equipment, no better results could be expected. The situation was all the more serious because more than half of the children of school age were educated under such conditions, which prevailed particularly in the rural areas.

It was clear to Bagley that the doctrine of local autonomy needed radical modification. This would have been desirable under any circumstance, but had become urgent with the new birth of national consciousness and unity brought about by World War I. It was also an inevitable corollary of "the new and pervasive comprehensive meaning for the word democracy," and the new status of the United States in the international world. A new nationalism demanded new policies to meet new needs. The conditions revealed by the draft showed the need to state a national aim to serve as a guide and to define standards for the development of an educational system that would preserve and strengthen the democratic ideal. The revelations of the draft pointed out that until the crisis of war served to arouse the American people, such matters as the rural schools, the preparation of teachers, health education, and the education of adult illiterates and of school leavers had been neglected. The existence of local inequalities in a wealthy nation had been brought to light. What was obviously needed was some official channel to define national policy, to stimulate local initiative, and to promote educational efficiency on a national scale. The American people must recognize that "it is just and equitable to tax the entire wealth of a community for the education of all the community's children." His arguments, in other words, pointed to the need of federal aid for education as the only way of meeting "a national problem . . . that transcends all state and local problems. We have an international obligation to discharge which will call for the highest level of enlightened intelligence in the body politic."

There was in Bagley's opinion another argument in favor of national policy and national support for education. In view of the different standards in the country, the number of immigrants, and the mobility of the people it was necessary to have a common policy to promote common interests and a common background of culture so that the American people could think and act together. It must be realized "that ignorance and mental sloth are much more than individual handicaps and misfortunes — that they are in a very real sense millstones around the corporate and collective neck of the body politic." Education is a steadying and stabilizing force as well as a force that contributes to national welfare and progress. Hence federal aid would be in the interest of the nation as a whole and at the same time would promote the effectiveness of state and local education. As to the fear of bureaucracy, Bagley believed that local interest and initiative were the best safeguard against it. Better educational conditions could be secured everywhere on a national scale without the danger of control or bureaucracy "if the people only say the word."[18]

In general Bagley and his collaborator, John A. H. Keith, president of the State Normal School, Indiana, Pennsylvania, presented a brief in favor of federal aid in their book, *The Nation and the Schools: A Study in the Application of the Principle of Federal Aid to Education in the United States*, which appeared in 1920:

> The book, in brief, is a collection of fact and argument designed to show that the Nation is, in a very real sense, an educational unit, that the Federal Government should assume a fair proportion of the cost of maintaining schools throughout the country, and that there should be established in Washington an adequate agency through which the educational needs of the Nation *as a Nation* may be made vocal.[19]

On the whole Bagley would probably have been content to have federal aid granted to teacher training institutions, an idea which he put forward first in 1915. It was as important to aid these institutions as it was to support land-grant colleges; the improvement of the facilities for the education of children was as important to the nation as methods for improving crops or raising hogs. Elsewhere he based his arguments in favor of aid to teacher training institutions on the analogy of the maintenance by the Government of institutions for the preparation of officers for the armed services, or of the federal aid provided under the Smith–Hughes Act for vocational education in high schools. "For the Government to cooperate with the states in doing this," he argued, "would be to recognize in a most effective way the much talked of dependence of the nation's welfare upon the public schools and the significance of the teacher's service to the nation's life."[20] Such subsidies would help "to establish standards [of instructional staff, library, laboratory facilities, and the like] which would insure adequate equipment, without exercising a bureaucratic influence which might prevent the best adaptation of these institutions to the needs of each state."

A summary of Bagley's position on the issue of federal aid is contained in one of his later discussions of the subject.

> In any event, there is a distinct need in the United States for participation by the Federal government in the *support* of schools. This would promote something akin to an equality of educational opportunity throughout the country, and the consequent protection of the stake that the people as a whole have in a literate, informed, and disciplined population. Ignorance within the national limits is not only a menace to local, state, or sectional welfare; it is a menace to national welfare.[21]

Because he wished to have official recognition given to education as a social institution analogous to agriculture, labor, commerce, and so on, he supported the proposal that a Department of Education be established with a Secretary as a member of the Cabinet. Such an establishment would help to promote national security and progress, and would provide educational leadership and lend prestige to education.[22]

In his criticisms of American education Bagley was always animated by his deep faith in education in general and by his conviction that through education the ideals of democracy could be strengthened. He recognized in the nation's provision of education a true manifestation of its idealism, and, despite its inadequacy on a national scale, he did admire the generous support given by the people at any rate for the fabric of education. Despite the shortcomings which he so often criticized, he was ready to admit that the school had contributed largely to the development of the likemindedness and homogeneity of the American people. The revelations of the draft pointed to serious defects that called for correction. Nevertheless, he did not deny that the morale of the American people was high during World War I and resulted from their common education. Above all he looked with pride upon the common school with its absence of class distinctions, and upon the expansion upwards of the universal school.

The essential characteristic of this expansion was the desire to implement the ideal of providing equality of educational opportunity to every boy and girl. Although he was ready to admit that the expansion was made possible by the country's wealth and became necessary as industrial processes changed from routine activities to activities requiring trained intelligence and adaptability, he believed that a far sounder justification could be found in democracy's need of highly trained citizens. No one was more aware of the problems that the upward expansion of the school system brought in its train.

> By far the most serious problem of American education today, in my judgment, is to provide kinds of instruction that will make it socially profitable to keep in school the types of young people who, under a simpler form of social and economic life, would be wage-earners by the age of fourteen, sixteen, or eighteen.[23]

He saw the necessity of differentiation of courses, but was opposed to premature differentiation to the detriment of the cultivation of common interests for all as future citizens to be engaged in common tasks.

Just as he was afraid of premature differentiation, he was equally opposed to the establishment of separate schools, differentiated according to purpose or the abilities of the pupils. In a famous debate with Dr. David Snedden he argued against the creation of separate vocational schools.[24] Although he recognized the danger to a democratic society of neglecting pupils of ability, he was opposed to the establishment of select schools for them and the inevitable encouragement of an aristocracy, even though it might be an intellectual aristocracy. He objected to any form of school organization that might result in social stratification.

> As a people we are pretty clearly committed [he said in the aforementioned debate] to the theory that talent is distributed fairly evenly among the masses and that it is the special prerogative of no special class or group. As a people, we are fairly firm in our faith that this latent talent may be trained to high efficiency in practically every case. We mean to keep open the door of opportunity at every level of the educational ladder. It is a costly process, but so are most other things that are precious and worth while.[25]

He did not surrender this belief, but he was greatly disturbed, as the expansion proceeded and the high school enrollments increased, by "the relaxation of standards," to which he frequently referred, and a tendency to level down and even to deprive competent students of the opportunity to pursue what he called "exact and exacting studies." The questions that he was disposed to ask as he saw this development were as follows:

> Can we realize the praiseworthy democratic ideal of equal educational opportunity for all without committing the American people to a standardized — an institutionalized — mediocrity? Can we maintain secondary schools that are quite unselective and higher institutions less selective than those of other countries and still compete with other countries in the development of talent that will be competent to the higher realms of intellectual activity?[26]

He did, however, recognize that "non-selective education is in no sense a substitute for the more highly specialized instruction and training of the gifted individuals of each generation."[27]

Bagley's objection to differentiation may be further illustrated by his criticism of the trend at one time to differentiate the aims of education for rural and urban schools and to give the rural child a narrower education for his prospective occupation. Not the aims but the environments differ and the duty of all public schools is to integrate all the diverse elements of the population.

The rural child as much as the urban child is entitled to be taught to see the meanings of the common things of life, and to appreciate his heritage, broad and liberalizing.[28]

In this fear of the danger that might result from differentiation through education may be found the key to Bagley's philosophy of education, whether in administration, theory, curriculum, or methods. The driving force throughout his career was his faith in the potentialities of the common man and the part that he should and could play as a member of a democratic society. At the same time he had a profound belief in the educative influence of participating in the affairs of a democracy. These views explain his constant insistence that the first function of education is to provide every future citizen with a background of common knowledge and information, common ideas and ideals, and a common sense of belonging in a community which transcends the individual and the immediate locality of residence.

It was also these views that determined his definition of the meaning of equality of educational opportunity. It was not so much equal access to schools that he considered to be central in this ideal, but the opportunity for every boy and girl to advance as far as his abilities would permit. In other words, he regarded the equalizing function as the most important aspect of the provision of equality of opportunity. This may sound like a cliché, but to Bagley the principle meant not just juggling with materials of instruction to suit the needs of each pupil, but a refinement of methods of instruction to enable all pupils to enter into their common heritage. The common essentials that encompass this heritage he insisted upon several decades before he came to be known as an Essentialist. Nor did he ever miss an opportunity to point out the dangers implied by the curriculum revision movement, which sought to adapt curricula to the needs of local environments. To this movement he was as much opposed as he was to having the materials of instruction emerge from the "felt needs" of the pupils. In both cases he felt that the people of America would be deprived of a common language of discourse and understanding, particularly since one of their characteristics is mobility which, so far as children are concerned, might mean a fresh start in whatever school they might enter.

Bagley's position on differentiation of any kind must be borne in mind when turning to a consideration of what was one of his most important and lasting contributions to American education — his courageous stand on determinism in education. The attack which he made, alone and in the face of the contemporary climate of opinion, was reasoned, cogent, and trenchant. Far more was involved in his criticisms of the application of the recently constructed tests to measure intelligence than the use to which they were put to determine the future intellectual, occupational, and social status of an individual. From Bagley's point of view the movement, if it spread and became established, would endanger the future of the common man, undermine the ideal of equality of educational opportunity, and lead to social stratification that would be inimical to the preservation of the ideal of democracy. He was moved more by these threats to the fabric of American life and institutions than he was by his interpretation of what the tests measured. The notion that he was out to attack the whole movement of testing and measuring, whether of intelligence or of achievement, was as fallacious as the notion that he was impelled by sentiment for the common man and the underprivileged. The extensive use of the IQ, as a measure of native endowment, he felt to be "fraught with educational and social dangers of so far-reaching a character as to cause the gravest concern." There was at stake a great ideal "that has already cost more in terms of human striving and sacrifice than anything else in the world."

His professional contemporaries were more disturbed by the attack on the newly won citadel which stood for the application of "scientific" methods to education and to the measurement of human traits. Bagley defined educational determinism as "the attitude of mind consequent on the conviction or assumption that the influence of education is very narrowly circumscribed by traits and capacities, which, for most individuals, are both innate and in themselves practically unmodified by experience or teaching." The claims made were that the IQ measured innate ability or native endowment and that mentality or intelligence is fixed and stable and the measure of it permanent and unchanging. These claims, he contended, were assumptions or hypotheses not based on facts. What was measured, he insisted and clearly proved, was not native intelligence but acquired intelligence, that is, a combination of native endowment and the influence on it of environment, experience, and formal education. The inferences drawn by the determinist from the assumption concerned Bagley more than the assumption itself. A determinist claimed that "the ability to learn" was limited in most persons, and since ability to learn was defined as ability to deal in abstractions, he concluded that those who had this ability were destined to become leaders, while the rest should begin vocational training as early as the sixth grade and prepare for careers as workers. The determinist, wrote Bagley, nonchalantly assumes that every man can be taught to know his own place and appreciate his own limitations, and mind his own business. Such a claim he regarded as antidemocratic, for in a democracy the task of education is not to train high intelligence but to train all for a high level of disciplined and informed intelligence as a basis for collective judgment and collective action.

It is more important in a democracy, argued Bagley, to devote wholehearted efforts to bring the masses of children up to a reasonable intellectual standard than to leave them ignorant and to train leaders. Processes of instruction must, however, be refined to educate all and to give them the chance of being able to share the understanding and to experience the work of gifted men. He did not maintain that he could make a Newton out of the common man by teaching him the principle of gravitation, but, to use his own words:

> I do maintain that I have enabled this common man in a very real way to participate in the experience of one of the most gifted men of all times; I maintain that I have given him one control over his environment substantially equal to that which this gifted man himself possessed. I maintain that in respect of this possession I have made this common man the equal of others who possess it. There are undoubtedly some men who could never grasp this conviction, but I should wish to refine my teaching processes far more than

teaching processes have yet been refined before reaching any fatalistic convictions as to where the line is to be drawn.

As one goes up the scale, Bagley believed that "education does tend in many ways to equalize individuals of varying abilities." This belief was based on the thesis that there are two types of growth: horizontal growth which is stimulated by such forces in the environment as education and experience, and which compensates in many important ways for the differences in the second type or vertical growth due to natural factors. Among the many investigations that he cited to prove his point that nurture plays an important part in making the most of nature and that the IQ is a measure of acquired intelligence, he showed that the results of the Army Alpha Tests, so often used to support the thesis of native intelligence, pointed rather in the direction of acquired intelligence. The results varied according to the strength or weakness of the educational systems of the states from which the draftees were drawn. One of the most telling points was the evidence which showed that the scores made by Negroes in the Army Alpha Tests were higher for those who came from Northern states than for those who came from Southern states. He also submitted evidence to show that when compared on their relative standing on ten counts "the states with the heaviest proportion of foreign-born inhabitants tend on all these ten counts to stand very high." He was able to demolish the Pro-Nordic Propaganda based on the results of the Army Alpha Tests put forward by Professor Carl C. Brigham in *A Study of American Intelligence* (1923). "The myth of Nordic-Aryan-*Herrenvolk* superiority" was a topic to which he returned in 1943 in the journal which he was then editing, *School and Society.*

Bagley was justified in including among the provisional conclusions with which *Determinism in Education* closes the following statements:

4. . . . . General intelligence is determined *in part* by environmental opportunities, especially by environmental pressures, and most profoundly in all probability by those types of environmental pressure that are represented by *systematic schooling* during the period of physiological growth or maturation.

5. The contribution of systematic schooling to general intelligence is probably equal to the combined contributions of native endowment and the informal pressures of the average social environment.

6. So powerful is the influence of systematic schooling that it appears in many ways to counteract some of the differences due to original nature, to such an extent at least that one is justified in referring to general intelligence as a human trait which "distills its own corrective" for organic variability, and in assuming that education may be made, in a very real sense, a "leveling-up" process. . . .

8. . . . In general, the school pressures that stimulate the learner to *systematic and sustained mental effort toward the mastery of relatively abstract processes and toward the formation of ever-broadening concepts in ever-widening fields of knowledge* seem to yield the largest growth.

9. It seems that the importance of *early* training, discipline, and systematic instruction can scarcely be overemphasized. "Educational opportunity" means with especial force care and culture during early childhood and youth.

Twenty years after he had begun his criticisms of determinism in education Bagley claimed that he had been right. In a criticism of other aspects of education that he considered weakening he wrote:

He recalls that just twenty years ago he was drummed out of the camp of the psychologists because he insisted that the IQ represented something that was not wholly predetermined in the genes. It seems now that he was right at that time – and he has a suspicion that he is right in his present contention.[29]

He had already had the satisfaction of noting the success which his attacks had met when he wrote:

It should be a source of gratification to know that the fatalistic interpretations of the intelligence-test findings, against which the present writer was one of the first publicly to protest as quite unwarranted by the facts, have been pronounced invalid by a series of investigations which have employed increasingly refined techniques.[30]

Bagley recognized the contributions of the mental measurement movement and the value of intelligence testing in diagnosing individual disabilities, grading pupils, and selecting for temporary jobs, but he deplored the extension of their use to determine the future of boys and girls. He entered the campaign primarily to defend the rights of the common man and the meaning of education for democracy. "A little more light for the common man this year," he wrote, "next year, or one hundred years from now, and the battle for humanity, for democracy, and for brotherhood is won." He objected to labeling anybody as superior or inferior, educable or ineducable, and to encouraging young people to believe that they were destined to lead or were incapable of leadership.

> If it is desirable that there should be more high IQ's among our effective leaders, the best way to get them, I contend, is to educate the rank and file justly to evaluate and select them rather than to imbue these gifted children with the notion that they have been Heaven-sent to lead their dull fellows.

His faith in the common man and his educability he expressed in the following words:

> It is my contention that the common mind of humanity has already demonstrated its ability to think for itself, that universal education can train it to think more clearly and in larger units — in any case that universal education can give it a common stock of dependable ideas with which to do its collective thinking — and that the first and foremost task of education is to do this job passing well.

He recognized, however, what was needed to do the job passing well, for he urged that

> Refinement of methods of instruction is the greatest need not only of the normal and subnormal, but also of the supernormal; and while the provision of a pervasive common culture is the prime function of democratic education, this does not mean an absolutely uniform curriculum, nor does it preclude an abundance of differentiation in what may be termed "non-essentials."[31]

The essential basis of Bagley's position on most of the problems of American education was his faith in the contributions that education could make not only to the preservation but to the strengthening and advancement of the ideals of democracy. It was this faith that determined his ideas on the important place of the public and of the teachers in the administration of education and on the importance that he attached to the education of the common man. He began to emphasize the place of the common elements in an educational program rather than differentiation, and collective thinking and action as more important than individualism as early as 1916. And he continued his discussions in this vein, for he felt that as the world situation was developing democracy was on trial. "A democratic society has a vital collective stake in the informed intelligence of every individual citizen,"[32] he wrote in 1938. Four years later, when war had already started, he insisted that:

> There is no reason why democracy cannot have a strong and virile educational system and still remain a democracy. . . . We can make American education strong and virile and a potent force in achieving our highly worthy ends. And unless present signs fail completely, that is precisely what we will start to do without delay.[33]

He was justified in his optimism, but the general revolt against the weakening practices at both the elementary and secondary levels, of which he had been the leading critic for over a quarter of a century, did not take place until after his death and after World War II had ended.

CHAPTER 4

RAISING THE STATUS OF THE TEACHING PROFESSION

BAGLEY FREQUENTLY STATED THAT, WHEN HE BEGAN THE study of education, he believed that the art of teaching could eventually be based on a sound body of laws and principles resulting from research and experimentation. Some day, he hoped in his early years, a science of education would be developed comparable to the sciences on which medicine and engineering were based. He expected that teaching, like these professions, would become an applied science. It was not long before he was disillusioned and had to admit that teaching and learning were too complicated for experimentation to yield predictive principles. He found that what he had formulated in 1905 as the "law of habit formation" was not irrefutable and was later superseded by the results from new experiments. Since he found that many other "laws," derived from experimentation, met with a similar fate, he turned his attention to another aspect of education, which he was to regard as the real key to its success.

That "the soul and substance of every school is the teacher" was by no means a new discovery made by Bagley. The axiom, "As is the teacher, so is the school," had a long history in the development of education. But since Horace Mann's days no educator had raised his voice as sincerely and as persistently as did Bagley, not only to improve professional standards and status, but to arouse public opinion to recognize their importance. He was convinced that no improvement in the teaching profession was possible until the people themselves desired a better status and higher rewards for teachers. He noted the singular paradox that the American public, which by tradition manifested a profound faith in education, had failed to realize the importance of better prepared and qualified teachers to give substance to their ideal.

It is possible that he had considered the problems of the preparation and the status of the teachers in the American system of education earlier, but there can be no doubt but that his attention was forcibly directed to them by the publication in 1911 of Lotus D. Coffman's study of *The Social Composition of the Teaching Population.* This was the first sociological analysis of the teaching profession in the United States and was conducted by a man who was later to become a colleague of Bagley's in the University of Illinois School of Education. Bagley was impressed with the details brought out in this study. He was to use these details frequently throughout his career, for they constituted the severest indictment — one of "the weakest links"[1] — of American education.

The predominant characteristics of the teaching profession, to which attention was directed, were the immaturity of the teachers generally, but more particularly in rural and village schools; the inadequacy or even lack of training; the short period of service, uncertain tenure, and mobility; the low status and poor salaries consequent on the low esteem in which the public held the teaching service; and the inadequacy of the normal schools in which teachers were being trained. Many of the teachers, he reminded the public and the profession, were too young to vote, although one of their most important tasks was to prepare boys and girls for citizenship. To these details was added another damaging fact that was frequently stressed by Bagley. He cited a statement, which appeared in a publication issued by the U. S. Bureau of Education, that, taking the country as a whole, less attention was paid to the preparation of teachers in the United States than in any other civilized country.[2] He was able subsequently to confirm this statement after visiting a number of European countries.

Bagley attributed the deficiencies that were revealed about the preparation and status of teachers to the fact that there were no recognized national standards for admission to normal schools and for certification. Most normal schools, even in the early years of the present century, were hardly more than high schools, and their curriculum consisted of little more than a review of the subjects of the elementary schools with some courses in methods of instruction. The standards of the faculties and the equipment of the normal schools did not compare with the standards in other state-maintained institutions. He hoped that the situation would be improved after the number of high schools began to be increased and higher requirements could be established for entrance to the normal schools.

In general, however, Bagley was inclined to place the responsibility for the low standards of the teaching profession on the public which remained obtuse to its importance as a primary factor in the success of the collective enterprise of education. The American tradition of local administration was largely responsible for the variation in standards. Except in urban areas, uncontrolled local autonomy was detrimental to the progress of education. There was a tendency in many local areas to nepotism, which meant the appointment of local girls with inadequate qualifications – in the long run, a saving of money on salaries since they could live at home. Nor was professional training a requirement in many states, where candidates could obtain licenses to teach on passing local examinations. Low standards of preparation meant low salaries, which in turn tended to make teaching a steppingstone – to marriage for women and to more remunerative occupations for men. If all the teachers were on parade, Bagley often pointed out, over half the number would pass in review before one could be found who had had the minimum of two years of training beyond the high school, had had three years of teaching experience, or had reached the legal age of maturity — twenty-one years. These facts justified the statement often made by Bagley that teaching was "not a profession but a procession." What disturbed him most, however, was the fact that about half the children in the country were being deprived of their rightful privilege of a sound education. The educational deficiencies revealed by the Selective Draft Service in World War I provided ample evidence to corroborate this.

An opportunity to verify the characteristics of the profession which the studies mentioned had brought to his attention came to him in 1917, when he was invited by the Carnegie Foundation for the Advancement of Teaching to participate in a study of the preparation of teachers in Missouri. Although responsible primarily for a study of the curriculum and for recommending proposals for its improvement, he could make his recommendations only in the light of the tasks that lay ahead of prospective teachers rather than on a doctrinaire basis. The breadth of his approach to the problems involved is indicated in the statement that "The education of the teacher is measured by the quality of the school, and that in turn has been almost unfailingly an index of the quality of the community." In the selection and preparation of teachers and in the way they performed their task in the classroom were bound up the hopes and ideals of a democratic society. This point was to be stressed, because it was apparently ignored by the public. "Taking the country as a whole," he wrote in 1929, "these institutions [for the preparation of teachers] have not as yet the measure of public respect and support that they richly deserve."[3] And in 1938 he was still able to write: "It is a curious and regrettable fact that the strategic importance of the institution preparing teachers for the lower schools has been so long in catching the imagination of the American people."[4] And yet as the agents of the public responsible for the preparation of future citizens, the process of helping them to do their work more successfully should have been a paramount consideration.

Bagley analyzed as follows the two views that prevailed on the organization of the curriculum for the preparation of teachers. The first, that of the liberal arts colleges, was to give the future teacher a general education with an emphasis on subjects to be taught and then to add separate courses on the theory and practice of education. The second view, that of the normal schools, was to construct a curriculum of academic and professional subjects with the needs of teachers in mind. A decided prejudice had grown up against the normal schools on account of their alleged superficiality and overemphasis on methods at the expense of mastery of subject matter, a prejudice which persisted long after Bagley mentioned it in the Carnegie report published in 1918. Although he regarded the prejudice as exaggerated and unwarranted, he concluded that "the situation that actually exists reveals the need of more definite agreement as to the kind and amount of 'broad scholarship' that a teacher should have."

Bagley addressed himself to this problem and produced one of his most important contributions toward a sound curriculum for the preparation of teachers. Looking to the future he may have had in mind a longer period of preparation than the two-year course of the normal schools. He always acted, however, on the principle "from practice to theory" rather than the reverse, which was a method more usually employed by his professional colleagues. Accordingly he recommended a reorganization of the curriculum which could be introduced in the two-year course of the normal school, but which could be applied in principle to longer courses. The recommendation of "professionalized subject matter" or "professionalized courses" will always be associated with his name as probably the most significant proposal for the professional education of teachers. The question for which he endeavored to provide an answer he stated as follows:

> Is it possible so to organize the content of elementary school studies that normal school students undertaking these courses shall not merely "review" previously gained knowledge, but rather acquire what will be substantially new views of familiar matter as well as much genuinely fresh knowledge? Can such courses induce a quality of mental effort and ensure a degree of mental growth equivalent to that which is implied in courses now recognized as of collegiate texture?[5]

Prospective teachers, in other words, should receive a liberal education with an emphasis on their future need and use of liberal studies as teachers.

The recommendation of professionalized subject matter was based on Bagley's desire to abolish the distinction between academic and professional subjects, and to secure greater attention in the normal schools to subject-matter courses and less emphasis on formal courses on professional subjects. Scholarship would not only not be diminished but would in fact be enhanced by a reorganization directed to professional ends of teaching in elementary or high schools. Moreover, subject matter and methods would develop together instead of being taught in separate compartments.[6]

Ten years later Bagley offered the following definition of the professionalization of subject matter. He described it as

> a really serious attempt to humanize knowledge, to reveal its true meaning, to show how it has evolved out of human experience, and how it has helped men and women to solve their problems, and especially to show how it can be built into the experiences of each incoming generation. As I conceive it, indeed, the whole purpose of professionalizing subject matter is to make sure that knowledge will throb with life and meaning, and that it will enrich in the largest possible manner the lives of just as many people as possible . . . to make knowledge really live in the lives of boys and girls.[7]

He may also have hoped that out of his recommendation would come a truce in the conflict already developing between academic subject specialists and teachers of professional subjects.

Bagley was conscious of the fact that his idea of professionalized courses would meet with objections, on the one side from academic subject specialists, and on the other from teachers of professional subjects. He realized from the start that the faculties of normal schools in general, and later of the teachers colleges which grew out of normal schools, were not competent or prepared to put his idea into practice. He was equally critical of the preparation of teachers in liberal arts colleges, where the academic subjects were taught separately and apart from the professional courses. For he was convinced that "techniques which are merely 'fastened on' to subject matter instead of growing out of the very nature and function of subject matter have not helped us much in the past, nor will they help us much in the future."[8]

To indulge in critical attacks without offering a constructive suggestion for the improvement of the situation attacked was not Bagley's way. He realized that to put forward an idea without showing what was needed to put it into effect was futile. He offered a suggestion well in advance of the time, but a suggestion which has an important bearing on other aspects of higher education than the preparation of teachers. As normal schools and teachers colleges advanced their standards to a collegiate level, a tendency to require a doctorate degree for instructors had developed. Salutary as this advance may have been, it did not correct the situation which caused Bagley's concern. The separation between specialists in academic and professional subjects was simply continued on a higher level.

A synthesis was proposed by Bagley to bring the two together in their common task of preparing teachers for public school service. His proposal was to prepare "teacher-scholars" to become instructors of future teachers. He drew a distinction between the "research-scholar" and the "teacher-scholar":

> The primary interest of the former is what may be called the vertical expansion of his subject field through the discovery of new truth. The primary interest of the teacher-scholar, on the other hand, is the horizontal expansion of his field — making its most important truths a part of the mental equipment of as large a proportion of the population as may be competent to learn them.
>
> This does not mean that the teacher-scholar is any less a scholar than his colleague whose chief interest is in research. He should, of course, be familiar through experience with the research methods of his field and he must keep up with the reports of those who are working on the frontiers. He differs from the research-scholar, in part, in that he must have a wide acquaintance with other fields, for one of his duties will be to show prospective teachers how his materials may be integrated with materials from other fields in the solution of significant social problems.[9]

The repeated emphasis by Bagley on professionalized subject matter and on the development of teacher-scholars was stimulated by his effort to meet the frequent criticisms that prospective teachers were inadequately prepared in the subject matter that they would be expected to teach and that too much time was devoted to training in methods of instruction apart from subjects. He realized that the future teacher needs a liberal education as well as a mastery of the subjects that he is to teach, but he felt that they should acquire this mastery in the light of their future professional needs. As early as 1917 he stated his views on the subject: "I am convinced that much of the so-called 'professional work' is generally futile, partly because it comes too soon and partly because it is unrelated to other subjects." The conception of professional work, he maintained, "must be extended to include specific courses in the subject matter that the candidates propose to teach, but courses organized from the standpoint of a relatively mature mind that is studying a specific teaching problem." Such an approach, he was to repeat frequently, would demand the same quality of thinking as the study of academic subjects of collegiate grade.[10] The teacher-scholar or subject-matter specialist would provide the balance needed by the educational theorist and "the so-called educational scientist." There was, of course, a place for those who could view the problems of education as a whole, but there was need of a great abundance of men and women teacher-scholars — "who know their specialized subjects in and out and all around, who love their subjects with a personal and passionate devotion, and whose chief aim in life is to get others to know and love their subjects."[11] There was a place for the applied science or technology of education but it was supplementary rather than central in the teacher's work.

When Bagley undertook the study of the preparation of teachers in 1917, it was already clear that he had abandoned his earlier expectation that the process of education could be based on scientifically derived principles or laws. From this time on the major qualifications that he regarded as most important in a teacher were his mastery of the subjects that he taught and artistry in teaching. Among the essential items that he listed in the equipment of a teacher were:

(1) thorough mastery of the material one studies; (2) a keen appreciation of the significance of these materials to human life; (3) an ardent desire to have others know and appreciate these materials; (4) a sympathetic understanding of the difficulties a learner will encounter in mastering these materials; and (5) a command of the technique by which these difficulties may be overcome.[12]

Bagley was rarely more eloquent than when he discussed teaching as a fine art and the teacher-artist. He believed that "the analogy of teaching with the fine arts is in many ways the most helpful of all," for it demands insight, intuition, sensitiveness to the learner's difficulties and sympathetic understanding of his needs, and an appreciation of the human heritage of knowledge, skill, ideals, and standards. "Like the painter and the composer, the artist-teacher will avail himself of whatever technology may be available, but his work is essentially a fine art, not a technological art."[13]

He had already begun to emphasize the aspect of artistry in his earlier writings. In his section of the Carnegie Foundation report on *The Professional Preparation of Teachers* (1918) he expanded his ideas and stated:

There is, of course, something of the applied science character in teaching, but fundamentally teaching is much more closely allied to the fine arts than to the applied sciences. . . . The painter, the musician, the writer, and the teacher might very likely do their job much better, if they possessed this knowledge of theory; but something other than understanding theory is assuredly the basic element in successful practice.

Teaching is not a mechanical trade but a fine art, and the teachers are not artisans applying certain tricks from applied sciences, but artists, and "the fine art of teaching is something more than a bag of tricks from which the clever craftsman can conjure successive miracles."

Bagley frequently deplored the apathy and indifference of the public about the preparation, qualifications, and status of teachers despite its professed faith in education. The public, however, looked for something tangible to show for the expenditure of the money that it provided for education. Bagley's reference to the backwardness of the United States in the matter of teachers as compared with other countries has already been mentioned. He regarded buildings, equipment, and even libraries as the shell of an educational system when compared in importance with the teachers. In the Carnegie Foundation report he described the teacher as the sole channel of influence as far as education through the schools is concerned. "The head and heart of this educative process is the direct and personal contact of a teacher's mind with the mind of the learner."[14]

The teacher is the primary factor in the making of a good school. But the influence of education goes beyond the school, for it is a process designed to contribute to the welfare and progress of society. Hence the function of the teaching profession is central and determining and the profession forms the keystone of the arch. Democratic institutions depend completely

> upon the enlightenment of the great masses of the people. . . . The hopeful fact is that government of the people by the people becomes stable and effective in proportion to the advancement that is made toward an effective education of the masses.[15]

Bagley often referred to the teacher's influence as a contributor to society's well-being and progress.

> Every teacher [he wrote in one of his early books] who comes in contact with the plastic material that we designate as childhood and youth can add a touch to this creative process — can influence definitely, tangibly, unerringly, the type of manhood and womanhood that is to dominate the succeeding generation.[16]

Despite the strategic importance of the teacher and despite a certain advancement of the status of the teacher's calling, which Bagley noted in 1929, there still prevailed a certain contempt for the teaching world, especially in the lower schools, and a patronizing attitude. He liked to illustrate the general attitude by his own experience. Once when traveling on a train a fellow passenger asked him what his occupation was. "I am a teacher," said Bagley. "A teacher?" exclaimed his questioner. "You must be about forty. What do you expect to make of yourself?" By that time Bagley had already made a world reputation for himself in the field of education! And there had been improvements in the number of trained teachers and in the length of service; standards of preparation had improved; and teachers in general were losing their sense of inferiority. The teaching profession was being gradually integrated and salary differentials between elementary and high school teachers were being reduced or even abolished in some localities. There had been a marked development of professional consciousness, an increase in the number and membership of professional associations, a greater concern for the study of educational problems, the creation of research divisions by state and national organizations, and an improvement in the technical literature of the profession. This development was confirmed in the reports of the National Survey of the Education of Teachers which were published in 1933 by the U. S. Office of Education. Bagley was a member of the board of consultants for the *Survey,* which was conducted by his colleague, Dr. Edward S. Evenden. Nevertheless in 1937 Bagley, after summarizing the report of progress presented in the *Survey,* was able to write: "The teaching profession still has far to go, however, before it meets the conditions that must be met if the schools are to discharge effectively the functions that are either implicit or explicit in the recommendations of the Commission [on the Social Studies]."[17]

In an article on "The University School of Education as a Source of Educational Leadership" Bagley attributed such progress as could be noted to the leadership of professors of education and the consequent raising of the standards for the preparation of administrators and supervisors for the public school services, of research workers, and of instructors for normal schools and teachers colleges. "Indeed," he wrote, "it is scarcely too much to say that the development of education in the United States has in recent years been guided by professors of education as it has been guided by no other group."[18] The "educational generalists," among whom he included professors of education, acquired an exclusive control of policies and programs for elementary and secondary schools. They acquired this control, as he frequently stated, by default, since the academic colleagues seemed to be unable to understand or refused to meet the needs of nonacademic pupils as the educational system expanded upward and the high schools became nonselective. The professors of education, who did not seem to be bound by the academic traditions, were ready to adjust programs to the different capacities of the pupils. The influence of subject-matter specialists and of scholars in the different fields of knowledge was gradually diminished in determining policies.

In making these statements Bagley sought to explain rather than to condone the growth of the influence of the "educational generalists."[19] He deplored the situation on several occasions. Thus in 1928, in discussing the conflict between subject-matter specialists and professional subject instructors, he said: "Much more serious than this, however, is the power and influence that the so-called professional groups practically monopolize in determining the work of the lower schools."[20] In another statement he pointed out what might happen as a result of this influence:

> Collectively, then, the professors of education exercise a measure of influence that is almost incalculable in its possibilities for good or for evil. Collectively they are discharging functions almost analogous to those that a responsible ministry of education would discharge under a highly centralized government. In a very real sense they are determining the course that American education is taking, and in the long run this is likely to affect profoundly the course that the nation will take in the future.[21]

Bagley's major contribution to the improvement of teacher preparation was his plea for the professionalization of subject matter. The plea was inspired in part by a desire to bridge the gulf which existed between subject-matter and professional subjects specialists. He was as much alarmed by the control over policies exercised by professors of education as were the critics from the academic side. But he was also animated by a still stronger desire to develop the art of teaching on a professional basis and to promote a certain independence of mind and freedom of action so far as was consistent with the task delegated to teachers by society. Teaching, he believed, required not only a background of liberal education and scholarly mastery of the subjects to be taught, but also a certain ability to adopt whatever method was indicated as most appropriate as a result of understanding, insight, and experience in the classroom.

While I am a professor of education [he once admitted in an address to a group of subject-matter specialists] and as such have perpetrated innumerable lectures and articles, as well as a few books, on methods of teaching, I have long been convinced that efforts to impose general patterns of teaching on diverse types of subject matter are not only of little avail but sometimes fairly disastrous. Good teaching procedures, in my judgment, must grow out of the subject matter to be taught rather than deduced from theoretical postulates and injected into subject matter by specialists in education.[22]

Professors of education were not the only objects of criticism because of their control of policies in general and on classroom activities; control of the teachers by supervisors and administrators was, in Bagley's opinion, just as objectionable. A most serious consequence of such control was the emergence of a hierarchy with the classroom teacher at the bottom. The contrasts between teaching, on the one hand, and supervision and administration, on the other, were sharply drawn and also constituted the line of professional promotion as the only method of rewarding successful classroom teachers. This overemphasis on "overhead" in American school systems was attributed by Bagley to an imitation in part of "big business which magnifies the executive functions." Under this system the school board corresponded to a board of directors, the superintendent to the general manager, his assistants and supervisors to foremen, and the principals to the bosses. The teachers had the status of "hands" or routine workers. Bagley began to criticize this situation in 1918 when, in an address before the N.E.A., he said:

The status of the classroom teacher is becoming more and more akin to that of the "hands" in a factory, working under foremen and superintendents who assume the real responsibility. More and more frequently, too, these foremen are being recruited from a group that has never served an apprenticeship in the actual work of teaching boys and girls. Schools, however, cannot be operated on the factory plan except at the peril of the vital and fundamental function that they must discharge.[23]

Teachers, he insisted, should have collective responsibility for educational policies in the making of courses of study, the selection of textbooks, and other matters, under the leadership of administrative officers.

He recognized, however, that only when they were well prepared as members of a profession could teachers be entrusted with responsibilities for policy making. When, some ten years later, Bagley reported the advances made by teachers, the increase in opportunities to participate in policy making and in curriculum construction, and the creation of teacher councils in a number of school systems were among the points that he noted. His faith in the well-prepared teacher who had a sound professional outlook and a sense of social obligation was unbounded.

> Given a reasonably high level of trained intelligence, the democratic group will be able to carry on even if competent leadership does not appear, and, although its progress may be slow, it is much more likely to be certain and sustained. . . . I have every faith that our profession will prove neither recreant nor inadequate to its great task and its great opportunity.[24]

Because he had faith in the teachers and was concerned about their preparation, he considered it an obstacle to progress that the only way a successful teacher could be rewarded was by changing his work instead of capitalizing on his experience to improve his status. This practice he regarded as a backward step "from the most exacting tasks to those which, while still difficult enough, really make smaller demands upon the individual." Under such conditions teaching could not acquire "the characteristics of a worthy life-career."[25] It is not without significance that Bagley always preferred to be known as a "teacher" rather than a "professor."

CHAPTER 5

BAGLEY'S PHILOSOPHY OF EDUCATION

IT IS DIFFICULT, FROM THE POINT OF VIEW OF ANY OF THE educational philosophies current in the twentieth century, to classify Dr. Bagley. Although he paid a striking tribute to William Torrey Harris and his work for the schools of St. Louis, he admitted that personally he was not always in sympathy with the teachings of Hegelian philosophy. He admitted further that perhaps this was because he had not always understood them.[1] When Herbartianism was popular, he never became a follower. When the child study movement and child psychology seemed to be the major preoccupation of educators, he never became the victim of sentimental adulation of "the child." When progressive education and pragmatism became dominant he stood out as the foremost critic of their manifestations in practice. He specifically denied that he was an idealist in the sense of transcendentalism; his emphasis on ideals and values no doubt was responsible for this classification. He refused to be described as a "traditionalist" which in the minds of many would rate him as an advocate of the *status quo* and an opponent of change under all circumstances. He proposed the name "Stalwarts" for the opponents of progressive education. "The Stalwart," he wrote, "makes systematic and orderly progress the central feature of his educational program."[2] In the last years of his career he came to be denominated an "essentialist," without regard to the fact that "essentialism" is not a philosophy, but stands rather for an emphasis on a point of view within a philosophy.

In the efforts to pigeonhole Bagley it was forgotten that he never claimed that there was only one way to salvation in education. Throughout his career and before progressive education became dominant he was always critical of attempts to find a "cure-all" and looked upon the succession of fads and innovations as detrimental to the cause of education. He refused to accept any particular philosophy as orthodox, no matter how distinguished its advocates, because he believed strongly that the advancement of education cannot depend on the direction of a monolithic doctrine. He feared that this would interfere with the professional freedom of the teacher who must face the complex problems that arise in teaching a classroom of pupils.

To understand Bagley's position it is important to bear in mind the various influences and experiences that contributed to the development of his intellectual and professional outlook. From his student days at the Michigan Agricultural College he acquired and always cherished a respect for the scientific attitude and method. This respect was confirmed and strengthened by his graduate training in experimental psychology at Cornell University. In the early days of his career he played with the idea of developing a system of education based on scientifically established principles on the analogy of medicine and engineering. It was not long, however, before he realized, probably from his own experiences in the classroom, that the practice of education involved more than an underpinning of scientific principles and that teaching — good teaching — had closer affinities to art than to the sciences. Bagley quoted with approval a statement by Henry Fairfield Osborn that "of all incomprehensible things in the universe man stands in the front rank, and of all incomprehensible things in man the supreme difficulty centers in human intelligence, human memory, human powers of discovery, research and the conquest of obstacles."[3] Bagley's faith in education was not shaken, but he was to grow increasingly skeptical of the extent to which education could be made into a science or even an applied technology.

Bagley's philosophical position was most clearly defined, not when he became known as the leader of the essentialist movement, but when he published his book, *Education and Emergent Man,* in 1934. This position he had already stated briefly in an essay on "Emergent Idealism" in *Education, Crime, and Social Progress,* published two years earlier:

> During the past two decades American education has been increasingly influenced by a psychology that is essentially mechanistic and a philosophy that, in its effects, is essentially opportunistic. The present essay and that which follows will attempt to prove, first, that a much more liberal psychological basis than mechanism provides, and an equally valid basis, can be made available for educational theory and practice; and secondly, that this psychological basis will justify a virile idealism in place of the weak opportunism that now prevails. A working hypothesis will be sought in the implications of emergent evolution when this now familiar hypothesis is used as a basis for interpreting the facts of mental life.[4]

Education and Emergent Man opens with a statement of the implications for psychology and educational theory of the idea of emergent evolution, an idea which had been fully developed by Lloyd Morgan.

> In this book [wrote Bagley] education will be regarded as a primary factor in that progressive accumulation and refinement of learnings which may be properly spoken of as social evolution. Since mankind is apparently the only animal species that is capable of accumulating and refining learnings and of transmitting them from generation to generation, education will be regarded as distinctly and uniquely a human prerogative. . . .
>
> *Evolution is a progressive series of integrations which reveal a clear-cut continuity of structures and an equally clear-cut discontinuity of qualities, properties, and in a certain sense of the term, functions.*[5]

It is from here on that his educational theory is explicated. Starting with the idea that social evolution is a characteristic of man, as biological evolution is of nature, he continues:

The hypothesis of the continuity of culture is of basic significance to those institutions of society the business of which is to see to it that the gains made from generation to generation are not lost to posterity. This is not to say that the preservation of the actual material products is the important thing (except in the case of written records); rather the important thing is the art or skill or knowledge that creates the material product.

The social heritage here implied

has two parts: (1) the material heritage of implement, utensil, machine, or any artifact or improvement wrought by Man and conserved over one or more generations for the use of Man; and (2) the spiritual heritage of tradition, custom, standard, ideal, knowledge, and skill.[6]

It was as instruments for the advancement of social welfare, progress, and evolution that Bagley from his earliest years in the profession insisted on the elements of man's social heritage as the essentials in education. And it was because he saw in the innovations, which he criticized almost from the start of the century, and particularly in progressive education, a tendency to ignore the essentials and to minimize the importance and value of the social heritage that he considered such movements inimical to the best interests of American society and of educational progress. There were, of course, many other reasons for his criticisms which will emerge as Bagley's views are presented, but in general it was the neglect of the social heritage as a basis for social stability and cohesion, on the one hand, and for new integrations, on the other, that disturbed him. In advocating the primary place of the essentials in the curriculum of elementary schools and of the "exact and exacting studies" in that of the high schools he wished each generation to enter into the social heritage which had proved its worth through the ages of man's strivings to understand himself and the universe in which he lived. He considered the social heritage to be each generation's capital which would acquire increments as new social needs and demands arose. In the essentials he saw the foundations from which social evolution would emerge.

This background, his abiding faith in education as a guarantee of social and human progress, and his confidence in the educability of the common man, explain Bagley's continued opposition to efforts to hasten progress by plans for revolutionary discontinuity or by the tendency to disparage or disregard tradition entirely. Throughout his career his familiarity with science and its development and his constant interest in the story of man's adventures in time and space (in history and geography) combined to give him a point of view which resisted the allurements of the new merely because it was new. Much may therefore be learned about his views on what education should be from his criticisms of progressive education or what, in his opinion, education should not be.

Bagley undertook at an early stage in his career what he later defined as the task of each individual – to identify the elements of weakness in American education and to make an effort to replace them with elements of strength. In his first book he entered upon his task with a criticism of some contemporary interpretations of the doctrine of interest.

> So long as the pedagogical doctrine of interest meant the following of the lines of least resistance, its failure as an educational principle was absolutely certain. Always to obey the dictates of interest, in this sense of the term, would mean the instant arrest of all progress. But if the interest means the desire for a satisfaction of acquired needs, the case is somewhat different. The child is no longer at the mercy of the strongest stimulus; sustained attention directed toward a remote end has become possible. But the point never to be forgotten is this: *acquired interests are developed only under the stress of active attention.* Always there must be some inhibition of natural tendencies at the outset. The passion for change, the insidious and often overwhelming desire to do something else must be strenuously repressed. . . . One vital necessity of education, therefore, is to develop *in the immature child* needs that will demand the acquisition of experiences *that will be beneficial in mature life.*

In criticizing the tendency to encourage pupils to browse around in sources and to nibble at this and that he insisted that "It is the function of the teacher to see that the various parts of the course are presented in consecutive order – in such a way that the pupil cannot fail to see the relations that the teacher desires to develop."[7] The results of child study were being abused as illustrated by the facts that "drill and discipline are obsolete, effort is discounted, there is less and less stamina, and a weakening of moral fiber."

A few years later he attributed the current trends in education to the social climate of the time. The statement, already cited in an earlier chapter, deserves repetition.

> Certain it is [he wrote in *Educational Values*] that the present tendencies in our schools toward ease and comfort and the lines of least resistance confirm rather than counteract the operation of that *Zeitgeist* which reflects so perfectly the moral decadence that comes with prosperity — the letting loose the grip that our forefathers, who lived under sterner and harsher conditions, had upon the ideals of self-denial and self-sacrifice.[8]

He deplored the disappearance of every kind of formalism from education, and believed that the criticisms of traditional practices and the doctrinaire proposals of new ones only confused and muddled the teachers in the classrooms. The child, on the one hand, occupied the center of the stage and received too much sympathy as the victim of education. The teacher, on the other hand, received none, although he was achieving something for the nation with inadequate rewards. Bagley did not decry the policy that school work should be made as simple and attractive as possible, but he did object to the policy which asserted vehemently that "the child should never be asked or urged to do anything that is not easy or attractive."

From the point of view of instruction the innovation which Bagley considered to be fraught with serious consequences was the abandonment of drill together with a disregard for training in the fundamentals. In a passage that deserves to become a classic in educational literature he made a plea for the right kind of drill:

> What is needed, now that we have got away from the lock step, now that we are happily emancipated from the meaningless thralldom of mechanical repetition and the worship of drill for its own sake — what is needed now is not less drill, but better drill. And this should be the net result of the recent reforms in elementary education. In our first enthusiasm, we threw away the spelling book, poked fun at the multiplication tables, decried basal reading, and relieved ourselves

of much wit and sarcasm at the expense of formal grammar. But now we are swinging back to the adequate recognition of the true purpose of drill. And in the wake of this newer conception, we are learning that its drudgery may be lightened and its efficiency heightened by the introduction of a richer content that shall provide a greater variety in the repetitions, insure an adequate motive for effort, and relieve the dead monotony that frequently rendered the older methods so futile. I look forward to the time when to be an efficient drillmaster in this newer sense of the term will be to have reached one of the pinnacles of professional skill.[9]

Bagley thus placed himself on record as a critic of educational panaceas which promised better results in education. His major criticisms of progressive education, when it became popular, were frequently repeated in articles and addresses. He noted an absence of a sense of direction or social aim and too much concentration on the individual in the expectation that he would somehow become a useful member of society if his education was based on the laissez-faire principle. There was in the movement no clearly defined curriculum but a blind reliance that something might develop through the encouragement of pupil initiative, experience, and activities which had their origin in the felt needs and immediate purposes of the individual. A stigma attached to planning a curriculum in advance lest something be imposed upon the pupil and result in indoctrination and authoritarianism. Fear of planning in advance was accompanied by opposition to systematic direction and pursuit of learning. The whole doctrine was founded on a misinterpretation of freedom, which became the means rather than the end of education.

Bagley was always ready to agree that progressive education had an important place in the early stages of a child's education, when the lines between work and play were not yet clearly defined. But beyond that the doctrine had only a limited field of application and would turn out to be unsound and unjust, particularly if propagated as an exclusive policy. As an expression of the contemporary cult of ease, comfort, and security, such a policy was based on ends that "are inimical not only to social progress, but to the welfare and especially the mental growth of the individual." On another characteristic aspect of progressive education which stressed the functional or instrumental value of knowledge Bagley's view was that "it neglected a function of knowledge which in comparison with the instrumental function is at least of equal importance," that is, the acquisition of a background for meanings. To the claim that the pupils in progressive schools acquired this background of knowledge, information, and skills incidentally, he objected that this could not be accomplished by "picking up painlessly various items of information" to the neglect of "system and sequence" in learning. He recognized some merit in the activity and project methods, but again refused to accept either as the only solution. For the curriculum based on activities and projects he had no use whatever.

What Bagley constantly deplored in progressive education was a tendency to follow lines of least resistance and least effort, which had been rationalized and sanctioned at the same time that drills, reviews, and systematic and sequential mastery of content were abandoned. To these trends he attributed the decline of rigorous standards, the flabbiness and superficiality in education, the softening and loosening influences, and the weakening of the moral and mental fiber. The emphasis which stood out prominently in progressive education was on the activity, purposes, and desires of the individual and on a cult of freedom without a sense of responsibility. As early as 1917, at the Portland meeting of the N.E.A., he read a paper with the significant title, "Are the Older 'School Virtues' Obsolescent?"

When extravagant claims were made for progressive education as a new and modern movement Bagley referred to the translation of an article by Karl von Raumer on "The Progressives of the Seventeenth Century" which had been published in Henry Barnard's *American Journal of Education* in March 1859. The article presented an account of a movement similar to the so-called modern progressive movement. He followed through by referring to the work of Rousseau and others whose doctrines favored child-centered education. Above all he objected to the claims to exclusiveness of the doctrine of progressive education put forward by its advocates and followers. As he wrote in an article in *Better Schools* in June 1939, "the greatest enemies of Progressivism are those among its adherents who have taken it as a religion and who are emotionally intolerant of everything that is associated with the educational order which they are seeking to change."

It is pertinent, perhaps, to synthesize Bagley's reasoned opposition to progressive education by presenting two quotations which may serve at the same time as an introduction to his own theory of education. After referring to the decline of rigorous standards in American education, he continued:

> In short, the net effect of these rationalized justifications of relaxed standards has been to open the paths of least resistance. The influence can even be traced in the changes that have taken place in our educational vocabulary. Practically every term suggestive of strength and vigor and rigor has been replaced by a weaker term. Certain words are seldom mentioned in our professional discussions except as objects of opprobrium – such words, for example, as discipline, thoroughness, and system.
>
> The educational practitioner and the educational administrator, in my judgment, have not been primarily responsible for these weakening tendencies. The spirit of the times has worked increasingly in this direction, and educational theory, in a very emphatic fashion, has compounded this influence.
>
> The extent to which these softening influences have gone is most clearly seen in the increasing vogue of what I shall call the Freedom theory of education. In its popular form, this theory deifies individual freedom, not only as an *end* of education, but also as the primary and most effective *means* to this end. Learning activities must not be imposed; they must always take their cue from the immediate desires and purposes of the learner. The continuance of the learning process must be justified at each step by the learner's own satisfaction with its results; as the street phrase has it, he must get a "kick" out of each learning experience. Imposed tasks and prescribed programs of study not only violate the inherent right of the learner to make free choices, but are themselves either futile or negative as educational means. Just now the favorite theme is the "creative impulse." By the simple legerdemain of "taking off the lid," it seems, one will be able to conjure creative products out of a vacuum.[10]

To this extensive summary may be added the following passage with which Bagley closed an article in the *Classical Journal:*

My own objection to Progressivism is that, in spite of many salutary virtues, it is at basis a weak theory. It lacks virility not in the sense that it is feminine but rather in the sense that it is effeminate. It is my contention that its virtues and worthy contributions to educational progress can be preserved without committing American education to its weaknesses and its shortcomings, especially at a stage of social evolution when education among the few remaining democratic nations needs most emphatically to be fused through and through with a virile and dynamic idealism.[11]

Bagley's concern for American education was not limited to the lower schools, although it was the effect and influence of so-called progressivism at this stage to which the major part of his criticisms were directed. He could not fail, however, to be disturbed by the tendencies in the area of secondary education, particularly after 1920, when the enrollments began to increase by leaps and bounds. In criticizing the developments in secondary education he remained loyal to the ideal of equality of educational opportunity as implemented in the common comprehensive high school. Nevertheless, he readily conceded that the difficulties of organizing an educational program at this level were increased in number and complexity as the school changed from its traditional place as a selective school to become nonselective. A curriculum that was suited to the abilities of a selected group of pupils was bound to prove unsuitable to the needs and abilities of a host of boys and girls differing greatly in intellectual capacities and interests. He realized that a relaxation or loosening of standards was inevitable as a measure to attract pupils and to keep them in school. But he could not condone the tendency to rationalize the relaxation of standards as a virtue and to introduce a vast number of new subjects or "learning experiences" because they were easy and appealing and made no great demand on intellectual effort.

The high schools were handicapped, on the one hand, by the lowering of standards in the elementary schools and the promotion of pupils from grade to grade on schedule. The practice of promotion on schedule was a consequence of Leonard Ayres's report on *Laggards in Our Schools,* published in 1909, which was taken to be a warning of the effects and the cost of retardation. A little later the practice was further encouraged by the psychologists' prediction of the dire consequences on the individual of failure and the stigma that then attached to the idea. The net result of the practice of promotion on schedule to avoid the stigma of failure was to pass pupils on to the high schools without mastery of the fundamentals, particularly of reading. The newer pedagogical theories, while they did not directly dominate the secondary schools, were responsible for the spread of attitudes of "get by" and "good enough." To these external factors could be added the practice within the schools of neglecting the brighter pupils and devoting most of the teacher's attention to the average and below-average pupils. It was generally assumed that the bright ones could look after themselves; instead of this they rested on "easily won laurels." Bagley's expectation, expressed in 1914, that the doors of opportunity would be kept open at every level of the educational ladder for all, including the talented pupils, was not fulfilled – not at any rate by direct help to the talented. "Our national experience," he wrote in 1937, "indicates that universal education on the secondary level can be socially a very expensive and a relatively ineffectual process."[12]

The target of Bagley's severest indictment of the trends at the secondary level was the attitude of educational leaders to the "exact and exacting" studies, by which he meant mathematics and physical sciences and foreign languages. The responsibility for the gradual displacement or even direct disparagement of these studies he placed on the academic specialists and on professors of education. The former showed a contemptuous attitude to the latter and ignored the problems produced by the changed character of the high school clientele; the latter, by default of the academic specialists, became the arch-protagonists of the nonselective high school and introduced subjects, activities, and learning experiences which were assumed to be better suited to the abilities and needs of the majority of pupils, assumed in turn to be incompetent to pursue academic subjects and waiting for something more palatable to them. Standards were relaxed and the subjects that constituted a liberal education went into a decline.

The process was rationalized by the protagonists on the basis not only of the fact of individual differences of ability, but also of an interpretation of the investigations of mental discipline and transfer of training conducted early in the century. It was convenient to conclude from these investigations that no subject in particular possessed a special virtue for mental discipline and that the idea of the transfer of training was exploded. Beginning with these premises, for which there was no justifiable warrant in the investigations, professors of education and administrators, eager to implement the ideal of equality of educational opportunity by an upward expansion of the universal school, started to disparage the exact and exacting studies and ended by discouraging able and competent students from taking them. At least twenty years before academic specialists showed any awareness of the situation as a result of the revelations of low academic standards during and after World War II, Bagley had written:

> The implications of the experiments on the transfer of training have been carried beyond the point justified by the experiments themselves and have been made the basis of a sweeping attack upon all subjects that are inherently difficult in the sense of being exact and exacting.[13]

The problem that confronts the nation today was defined by Bagley as far back as 1930:

> The flabbiness and superficiality of American education are due to the lack of adequately prepared teachers, not only in elementary schools but on the secondary and higher levels as well — a condition almost inevitable in view of the rapid growth of the high schools and colleges. The larger problem is: Can schools and colleges level up instead of down? Can we realize the praiseworthy democratic ideal of equal educational opportunity for all without committing the American people to a standardized-institutionalized-mediocrity? Can we maintain secondary schools that are quite unselective and higher institutions far less selective than those of other countries and still compete with other countries in the development of talent that will be competent to the higher realms of intellectual activity? Finally, throughout the range of school and college life can we make the education of all an effective stimulus to intellectual and volitional growth upon the part of all?[14]

The withdrawal of the academic specialists from active concern with the developments of their own special fields of interest and the gradual decline of participation in the affairs of secondary education disturbed Bagley considerably. It was not only their position on the secondary level of education that he regarded as inimical to progress, but also the lack of balance that was developing in the subjects of the elementary schools because of the decline of cooperation between the academic specialists and professional educators. To the value of such cooperation Bagley could give personal testimony from his own collaboration with Professor Charles A. Beard in the preparation of school textbooks in the field of history. He noted on several occasions the fact that academic specialists did not participate in the preparation of yearbooks on special subjects.

This separation between academic specialists and professors of education became particularly marked when what Bagley referred to as "the curriculum revision jamboree" was launched in the 'twenties. Curriculum experts sprang up overnight and curriculum committees were created in many parts of the country and operated under the direction of the experts. Generally both the experts and the committees tended to ignore or to minimize the importance and need of common elements of culture and of a certain basic uniformity of content in the educational systems of a democracy. In 1932, as Bagley frequently pointed out, the library of Teachers College, Columbia University, had a collection of 30,000 curricula, each apparently "built" to suit the needs of a local community. The effects of such variety of educational practices upon the children of a people characterized, as the American people were, by their mobility were disregarded. In general the tendency was to reject traditional subjects and to add new materials of instruction, which had not been tried out but "sprang full-fledged from the fertile imagination of curriculum reformers." All types of innovations and objectives were proposed – new groupings and regroupings of subjects, activities and problem approaches, new aims and attitudes were recommended. A place was found for everything except systematized and sequential learnings which were described as nothing more than "mere knowledge." The chief measure of value was the immediate function or the usefulness of what might be learned, and not infrequently the pupil was to determine the value of an activity in the light of his own felt needs.

Bagley's own philosophy of education could almost be reconstructed from his criticisms of most of the trends that were manifested during his career. His skepticism about fads and innovations has been described earlier and in detail. It seems to be the fate of the critic, particularly in American education, to be regarded not only as an opponent of all that he criticized but sometimes as an enemy of education deliberately intent on interfering with its progress. Rarely is any effort made to discover whether behind the criticisms there exists a profound and constructive philosophy. This is the fate that befell Bagley who in his own quizzical way stated on one occasion that he would rather be right than respectable, and on another occasion that he would rather be right than progressive. In 1939 he referred to himself as "an educational theorist who has usually been out of step with many, if not most, of his colleagues in the field." He found himself, as he stated in 1932, assuming a much humbler role than that of setting on foot new fashions in education, "but perhaps in the end an equally significant function — namely, salvaging from the scrap-pile and preserving for the future the valuable elements which almost every one of these fashions represents — often, I admit, in microscopic amount, but worth saving none the less."[15] If he was not daunted by the attacks and at times the ridicule with which his position was assailed, nor by being "drummed out of the group of psychologists," as he recalled, it was because he was confident that his theory was based on facts and realities and that his educational principles grew out of practices in the classroom.

In his criticisms of innovations and new fashions in education he was concerned by the shifting values and indefinite aims. A clue to his position can be found in the following sentences which appeared in his first book:

> What we need in education is something definite to tie to. If this something be accurate and exact, so much the better; if it cannot be accurate and exact, let it approach this ideal as closely as possible, but

in any case let it be definite. If we have a definite notion of what we are trying to accomplish, and if we realize that this notion is subject at all times to the changes that later discoveries may necessitate, we shall at least have a chance to make some degree of progress and yet escape the danger that is incident to hasty generalization.[16]

It was perhaps an element of strength in Bagley's theory of education that he early formulated a definite aim for education by which he guided both his critical and constructive pronouncements. A number of ideas constantly recur with renewed emphasis throughout his writings and addresses. If he was opposed to giving pupils the initiative in deciding what they would like to study, or to building a program of studies on the basis of their felt needs or of their problems of the moment, it was because as a psychologist by training he believed in the educability of man owing to his early plasticity and his capacity to profit from past experiences. Such experiences should, he believed, serve to modify inherited adjustments and contribute to the formative task of education. The school he considered to be a specialized agency that should control these experiences and give direction to definite ends. "The task of selecting for survival the essential elements of experience is one of the most troublesome constructive problems of the educator." Hence "To see to it that the ideals which accumulated human experience has shown to be worthy and to make for social welfare are safely and effectively transmitted from generation to generation is obviously a prime task of education."[17]

The capital in which the materials of education are to be sought is the experience of the race or the social heritage.

The first question for which we should seek an answer in connection with the value of any subject is this: How does it influence conduct? . . . If there is one thing upon which we are all agreed to-day it is this: that it is what our pupils do that counts, not what they know. The knowledge that they may possess has value only in so far as it may directly or indirectly be turned over into action.

Let us not be mistaken upon this point. Knowledge is of the utmost importance, but it is important only as a means to an end — and the end is conduct.[18]

Knowledge, in other words, must be functional or instrumental, but in a larger and richer sense than was later implied by the pragmatists or instrumentalists in their use. Indirectly, for example, knowledge could serve as background that influenced conduct and attitudes.

In the process of selecting materials of instruction out of the rich heritage of human experience "an irreducible minimum" is set by society, which demands that the product of the school shall be able to "read, write, and cipher." When the minimal requirements demanded by society have been met, the teacher, like the artist, has a larger scope for his creative talents.

> But the finished product of the teacher's art must be more than a reading-writing-ciphering automaton. It must represent a highly complex mechanism of civilized habits, delicately adjusted to respond effectively to the innumerable stimuli of an increasingly complex social life. It must represent a storehouse of organized race-experience, conserved against the time when knowledge shall be needed in the constructive solution of new and untried problems. It must represent the initiative that is competent to adapt means to ends in the solution of such problems. And, beyond all this, it must represent ideals – those intangible forces that can lift a race in a single century through a greater distance than it has traversed in all preceding ages. Every teacher who comes in contact with the plastic material that we designate as childhood and youth can add a touch to this creative process – can influence definitely, tangibly, unerringly, the type of manhood and womanhood that is to dominate the succeeding generation.[19]

In his earliest writings Bagley recognized the schools as an agency created by society to carry out certain demands imposed on it by society. The selective draft during the years of World War I not only re-enforced and confirmed this belief but also brought to a focus the contributions that the school ought to make to society's welfare and progress. The data collected during these years revealed the defects and shortcomings of the American system of education. It brought to light the large number of young Americans who could not read and who had physical defects. A not inconsiderable number was discovered who could not speak the English language and were not only ignorant of the history and ideals of American life and institutions, but still continued to be reared in and devoted to alien ideas and ideals. Much of the responsibility for these conditions Bagley attributed to the ineffectiveness of localism in the provision and administration of education. "An educational system in a democracy," he believed and frequently stressed, "has a fundamental duty to discharge in insuring a thoroughgoing community of ideals, aspirations, and standards of conduct," so that the citizens can think and act together. He maintained "that ignorance and mental sloth are much more than individual handicaps and misfortunes — that they are in a very real sense millstones round the corporate and collective neck of the body politic." Education must be considered "a bulwark of the social structure,"[20] or, as he put it on several other occasions, education should be a stabilizing force for society.

It was for this reason that he always stressed "the fundamental significance of having among all of the citizens of a democracy a common basis of habits, ideas, and ideals" instead of the aim inherent in programs proposed by reformers of content that appealed and was attractive to each individual.[21] In the race between education and catastrophe he maintained that "If education is to save civilization it must lift the common man to new levels — and not so much to new levels of industrial efficiency as to new levels of thinking and feeling." The prime function of education in a democracy is to provide a *pervasive common culture,* which in his opinion, "does not necessarily mean an absolutely uniform curriculum, nor does it preclude an abundance of differentiation in what may be termed 'non-essentials'."[22]

The vast majority of pupils could be given a share in that pervasive common culture, provided that the methods of instruction were refined and adapted to the differences of ability, which must be taken into account. He pinned his faith on the education of the masses as an agency in stepping up mass intelligence, and, as previously mentioned, he relied more on the collective judgment of the common man than on the leadership of the talented. Further, such education would serve as a stabilizing force at a time when many forces in the country were making for instability.[23]

A community of culture, a common core of ideas, meanings, understandings, and ideals, representing the most precious elements of the human heritage, is demanded in a democracy. A democratic society has "a vital stake in the informed intelligence of every ctitizen," and a literate electorate is indispensable for its welfare and survival.[24]

In contrast to what he considered to be the vague generalizations and expectations of those who stressed the needs and interests of the individual without a clear sense of direction, Bagley at all times emphasized the social aim. The society that he always had in mind was the American democracy. Accordingly, he often referred to

> the complete dependence of democratic institutions upon the enlightenment of the great masses of the people. . . . The hopeful fact [he wrote] is that government of the people by the people becomes stable and effective in precise proportion to the advance that is made toward an effective education of the masses.[25]

On the eve of World War II he repeated the idea in another form when he wrote that "the primary function of American education is to safeguard and strengthen the ideals of American democracy" and to develop democratic discipline "that will give strength and solidarity to the democratic purpose and ideal" to meet the competition of and conflict with totalitarian states.[26]

The social aim and social efficiency were uppermost in Bagley's mind in a period when reformers and innovators were devoting their major attention to *the child* or to the individual and his needs. In discussing the controls of conduct he considered "the standard of social efficiency as the norm to which questions of this type shall be referred." A few pages later he again emphasized the same idea: "It is hard to see why the social criterion should not have the position of primacy in a rational theory of education. It is true that the race is composed of individuals, but it is also true that the individual has always been subordinate to the race."[27] Social efficiency, he had already pointed out earlier, implied ability to earn one's livelihood or "to pull one's weight," with as little interference as possible with the efforts of others, and readiness to contribute to social progress.

The standard of social efficiency must be rigorously applied to the products of the school. The school must fit the individual, not for the life of the past, nor for a remote Utopian future, but for the immediate future, the requirements of which can be predicted with reasonable certainty. If it fails to do this, the school cannot justify its existence.[28]

In one of his later books he stated that "the development of the democratic principle justifies the term 'society' in the sense of 'all the people' as the antithesis of the term 'individual'." He then proceeded as follows:

In this usage of the two terms the position taken in this book is that the interests and welfare of the social group are of primary significance. Both common sense and the history of mankind, however, coincide in the conclusion that the interests and welfare of society are best served by recognizing a wide range of individual "rights" and "liberties," which, under the peace-code, are guaranteed by the social group.[29]

The conduct of the individual in the interests of society and of social efficiency should, Bagley maintained, be guided by ideals. It would be difficult to overestimate the importance of ideals in civilized life; they serve as standards and criteria for conduct in the realization of purpose, and in order to be effective they must have a powerful feeling behind them.[30] Ideals form part of the eternal and fundamental values which the teacher should help his pupils to recognize.

For the great triumph of teaching is to get our pupils to see the fundamental and the eternal in things that are seemingly trivial and transitory. We are fond of dividing school studies into the cultural and the practical, into the humanities and the sciences. Believe me, there is no study worth the teaching that is not practical at basis, and there is no practical study that has not its human interest and its humanizing influence — if only we go to some pains to search them out.[31]

Ideals, however, represent only one type of serveral outcomes of education. In *Education and Emergent Man* Bagley repeated an earlier classification that he had made of the outcomes of learning in which the following four categories were employed:

(1) Habits and skills. (2) Knowledge: ideas, concepts, meanings, facts, principles. (3) Ideals and emotionalized standards. (4) Attitudes: (*a*) primarily intellectual (points of view, mental backgrounds, perspectives); (*b*) primarily emotional (appreciations, tastes, loyalties, interests, prejudices).[32]

The important part that the school could play in developing character Bagley succinctly stated in an address delivered in 1917 at the meeting of the N.E.A., when he said, "What we sow in schools to-day, will be reaped in the next generation." Nor was he afraid, as were those who espoused other theories of education, that the older school virtues of obedience, discipline, duty, persistent effort, and thoroughness of mastery and workmanship would militate against the development of the initiative and originality of the pupils.

Not the least important of the ideals that he emphasized was the ability to control immediate desires and wishes in favor of remote ends. He was convinced and often repeated that

The essence of civilization is that *remote* and not immediate pleasures govern conduct; *remote* and not immediate ends determine action. And the capacity of man to govern his conduct by remote ends *depends entirely upon a process of education.*

And a few pages later he stated that

Not activity alone, but sustained and directed activity has been the keynote of human progress. Individually it expresses itself in unremitting effort toward the attainment of a far-off goal. Psychologically it means the subordination of inherited impulses to remote ends. In popular language, it is the expression of "will-power" or "self-control."[33]

He was able to meet attacks on the theory of effort by such arguments.

Carrying the idea over to training in conduct, he stated that the end of both external discipline and self-discipline is

to control conduct either with reference to relatively remote ends or consistently with worthy regulative ideals, *and in the face of immediate impulses, interests, and whims whenever and wherever these are inconsistent with the ends or the ideals in question.*[34]

He feared that the contemporary doctrine of interest was naïve, because

It encourages the attitude which waits for work that attracts, and discourages the appropriate and only rational attitude toward work — namely, putting forth the effort to *make the work attractive.* It makes one the slave of one's desires and enthusiasms rather than their *master.*[35]

He frequently insisted on a principle, which he had learned from his own experience, that tasks which initially may not be appealing or attractive may yet lead to gripping and enduring interests. Frequently efforts are sustained only in the face of immediate desires. A regimen of order and industry for sustained effort are traits that the race learned very slowly, but fundamentally are essential to social progress.[36] Without effort and application he believed that desired and lasting results could not be achieved. "Learning merely for the sake of the immediate (and very likely unimportant) application, unless accompanied by this 'intent to remember,' would seem to be a superficial learning."[37]

The notion that Bagley stood for a return to traditional practices is nowhere so clearly disproved as in his discussion of the two topics of discipline and freedom, which he always linked closely together and associated with his views on effort, social efficiency, and democracy. He was as much opposed to the harshness and rigidity of the past as any reformer or innovator who made a fetish of freedom, initiative, and individuality. He never abandoned the principle that the function of education is to develop in the individual conscious controls of conduct, which he regarded as fundamental to the development of self-discipline and the attainment of freedom. He was always consistent in his opposition to the practice of what he called "the dominant theory" of giving immature pupils freedom whether in the choice of studies or in their moral development.

While the conduct of the child must be brought into harmony with the ideals of the teacher (which in turn represent the ideals of that larger society for participation in which the child is being prepared), the modern conception of discipline would bring the child as rapidly as possible to the point where he will recognize the necessity of repression, and see clearly that the demands made upon him, and the limitations placed upon his conduct, are really dictated by something more fundamental than the arbitrary will of those in authority.

The newer conception of discipline, in other words, recognizes that the measures which the school must take to control its pupils should serve as far as may be to illustrate the basic necessity for law and order in a civilized society.[38]

The democratic ideal, he was to write more frequently as it began to be threatened from without, requires for its security and survival the gradual development of self-government, freedom, and responsibility. Freedom is won by the individual when he has so demonstrated his ability to stand alone that external discipline can cease. The dualism between discipline and freedom is resolved, according to Bagley, when it is borne in mind that "disciplined freedom" is a function of maturity; or, as he phrased it elsewhere, when "responsible freedom" becomes an end in education. True freedom is always a conquest, never a gift. The motto that he proposed for an educational theory "meet for the needs of democracy in an increasingly industrialized civilization" was "Through Discipline to Freedom."[39]

That his theory of freedom and discipline was not merely a matter of educational philosophy but a reflection of what Bagley regarded as essential to the welfare and survival of democratic institutions was clearly demonstrated in the following passage:

The vital importance of discipline to democracy is likely to be discounted and obscured by irrelevant appeals to "freedom" — and its implications of ease and comfort. Unless democracy can find a place in its theory and practice for discipline, duty, and sacrifice, it will be so seriously handicapped that its ultimate success will be a matter of the gravest question. Whether we like it or not, we cannot deny that, in the history of the race, anything that even remotely resembles freedom (freedom not only from personal thralldom, but freedom as well from want, dread, fear, fraud, and superstition) has been a conquest, not a gift. In a very real sense, education must reflect in each generation this element of struggle and conquest.[40]

Democratic discipline and responsible freedom are essential to "give strength and solidarity to the democratic purpose and effort" in the conflict with totalitarian states.

Bagley always described the looseness and flabbiness of American education as the results of reformist theories which brought discredit on the concepts of freedom and discipline as much as they did on the content and methods of instruction. He never ceased to plead for "iron in the blood and lime in the bones" of education as a protection against the softening sentimentalism that prevailed. He had begun to emphasize the need of vigor and virility in the educational system as early as 1916, when in an address at the meeting of the N.E.A. he said: "In my opinion, the time is ripe for a little tincture of iron in our educational philosophy, for a renaissance of thoroughness and a reasonable measure of rigor, for something approaching a revival of the ideals of duty and effort." An educational theory to meet the needs of American society "must be strong, virile, and positive, and not feeble, effeminate, and vague."[41]

There was no break in gauge in Bagley's philosophy; he emphasized social efficiency as the goal of education and his concept of the curriculum was directed to the achievement of this goal. Both were directed to ensure the stability and survival of society as well as of the individual who was to learn to live in it and contribute to its welfare. His major objection to the new trends in education was that their aim was marked by vagueness and uncertainty about what was to be taught. He insisted at all times throughout his career on the importance of system and sequence in the arrangement of the program of studies instead of improvisations determined by the felt needs and problems of the pupils. He felt strongly, when he criticized the new theories of curriculum making, that "to discard system and organization entirely is to repudiate the basic law of all advancement; evolution is simply a progressive development toward forms that are more and more elaborately organized, and in which system and coherence take the place of chaos and incoherence."[42] When, in 1911, he had occasion to discuss new methods in the teaching of reading, he insisted that "to learn to read, however, requires systematic instruction of a rather strenuous nature," and prophetically anticipated the answer to the question that was to be raised a generation or so later in "Why Johnny Can't Read."

Teaching without system and sequence and by informal methods and incidental learning disregarded the internal relationships of a subject.

He stated his own position clearly when, after referring to the practice of deriving the materials of learning from the felt needs or interests or problems of the pupils, he wrote:

> The systematic and sequential mastery of past experience as organized in the various fields of human inquiry I regard as the most dependable source of helpful backgrounds. It is easy to deride such mastery as the accumulation of mere knowledge; it is easy to deride the learning processes that demand effort and sustained attention in the face of desires and distractions. One may be sure that any proposal that sanctions and ratifies the lines of least resistance will receive the applause both of the gallery and a goodly section of the pit. . . . To read out of the picture systematic and sequential learnings based upon the logical, chronological, and causal relationships of the materials of learning is not only to obscure the importance of dynamic and dependable mental background; it is to encourage an ineffectiveness which has been clearly apparent wherever the theory in question has been applied consistently on a large enough scale to show how it works.[43]

Bagley's position on the matter of the curriculum, as of his educational philosophy, can best be understood in the light of the concept of emergent evolution which always influenced his thinking, although he did not explicitly enunciate it until the 'thirties. It was in the spirit of this concept that he believed that curriculum materials could best be found not in the immediate needs of individuals or of contemporary society, but in the experience of the race. Humanity through the ages had sifted out and selected what was most valuable for the use and the survival of the race, and left that experience as the cultural and social heritage for subsequent generations to preserve, modify, transmit, and enrich as changing circumstances demanded. As a student of history he recognized the fact that human experience must inevitably change and be modified. What aroused his opposition was the tendency to change for the sake of change, and to assume that all change is always for the better and means progress. He valued the backgrounds acquired from the study of race experience not least because they served as a protection or safeguard against hasty generalization.

Beyond the tools that it supplies, race experience, he believed, provided an equipment for life in the form of backgrounds which determined perspectives, attitudes, points of view, and standards of taste that serve as guides to conduct. Out of the body of race experience or the cultural heritage the subject matter that makes up the curriculum of schools is selected and gives meaning and significance to the world in which we live. Hence, he felt, education should transmit the lessons from human experience that are most useful and valuable for social welfare and progress and at the same time for the equipment of the individual to become a member of society. The organization of these experiences into subjects is not arbitrary or illogical, for, as he put it,

> Throughout the curriculum of the school, then, each of the various branches of knowledge really represents a certain type of experience with a limited phase of the world about us or within us . . . a recognition of the arts as well as the sciences, of doing as well as knowing, of action as well as thought.[44]

Each subject accordingly stands for a certain specific attitude toward our environment.

In an address on "Education and Utility," delivered in 1909, he stated that the ordinary subjects of the curriculum included

> reading and writing and arithmetic, geography and grammar and history — those things which, like the poor, are always with us, but which we seem a little ashamed to talk about in public. Truly, from reading the educational journals and hearing educational discussion to-day, the layman might infer that what we term the "useful" education and the education that is now offered by the average school are as far apart as the two poles.[45]

He attached special importance to mastery of reading, measuring, and computation for the conservation of linguistic and numerical literacy. "Reading must be accorded supreme importance from the point of view of direct utility," and the subject requires systematic instruction of a rather strenuous nature. Since the art of study consists of ability to assimilate the experiences of others, or, as he called them elsewhere, vicarious experiences, the problem is, "How may pupils be trained effectively to glean, through the medium of the printed page, the great lessons of experience?"[46]

He did not develop an elaborate classification of subjects in order of importance. The basic criterion of the value of a subject was to be found in the answer to the question, "How does it influence conduct?" and the chief value that he attached to knowledge was as a means to an end, and that end was, in his opinion, conduct – both practical and intellectual. Among the educational materials that should be included to attain this end he recommended history and biography, literature, the arts, and religion.

> The true function of national history in our elementary schools [he wrote] is to establish in the pupils' minds those ideals and standards of action which differentiate the American people from the rest of the world, and especially to fortify these ideals and standards by a description of the events and conditions through which they developed.[47]

To history he added geography, the one to extend the time perspective of the pupils and the other to widen their space horizon. "Both subjects are useful for intelligent participation in the solution of collective problems of citizenship," and to lift the pupils above the confines of the local and immediate.[48]

Bagley did not share the opinion that was general about social studies, namely, that "they are superior, assimilable, and functional for everyone in the discharge of responsibilities as a citizen." He regarded the social studies as "the primrose path of least resistance," bolstered by slogans "with limitless potentialities in an age when high-sounding shibboleths, easily formulated, can masquerade as fundamental premises and postulates wrought through the agony of hard thinking."[49]

For education in citizenship Bagley considered the study of history and geography to be more valuable than the social studies. To these subjects he added sciences which "are in themselves in the last analysis social sciences *par excellence*." He considered that to almost everyone living under modern conditions knowledge of the elementary principles of physics, chemistry, and biology, and of their simpler applications in the technologies of mechanical and electrical engineering and in technologies of sanitation and hygiene has a direct, practical, utilitarian value — the kind of value that is measured in dollars and cents. Far beyond this, however, are the needs of every citizen for a background of scientific knowledge that will enable him to participate intelligently in the collective decisions that a democratic society must make regarding a multitude of political and social problems.[50]

The transition from the theory of the curriculum for elementary schools to that of high schools followed naturally. Bagley did not turn his attention to the high schools until their enrollments increased rapidly after World War I. He realized that the traditional studies of the academic curriculum required types of ability and interest that many pupils did not possess, but he deplored the tendency to follow the lines of least resistance and to expand the list of "offerings" in the hope that among them the so-called nonacademic pupils would find something that they felt suited their needs and interests. He lived long enough to see the lists of which he was critical expanded beyond the point where they could be justified on educational grounds. For this condition, as pointed out earlier, he held both the professors of education and the academic specialists responsible. The former recognized that the problems of the high schools had changed as the schools changed from selective to nonselective institutions. But that did not justify the professors of education, in Bagley's opinion, in ridiculing the value of the academic subjects, or, as he called them, "the exact and exacting studies," and beyond that in disparaging and discrediting them. The academic specialists allowed the situation to go by default, because they showed no concern for the problems of the high schools and did nothing to assist those interested in preserving the exact and exacting studies.

The professors of education, as the protagonists of the nonselective high school, as the expansion upward of the universal school developed, sought to adjust the courses wholly to the needs, interests, and aptitudes of the pupils. They based their innovations on the rejection of the doctrine of formal discipline and transfer of training. They regarded all subjects as of equal value from the point of view of mental discipline. Bagley, however, was convinced that "the implications of the experiments on the transfer of training were carried too far beyond the point justified by the experiments themselves, and have been made the basis of a sweeping attack upon all subjects that are inherently difficult in the sense of being exact and exacting."[51] The expansion of the curriculum offerings was accompanied by a relaxation of standards to such an extent that "the term 'high school graduate' means little more than that a person so designated has passed through a period of secondary education of a standardized duration."[52] One definite result that was frequently noted was that the exact and exacting studies were gradually pushed into the background. The importance of studying mathematics, sciences, and foreign languages was belittled and exact and exacting studies were discarded as not functional or applicable in a specialized occupation and no longer useful for mental discipline. Even students who were competent to pursue them were discouraged from taking these studies. Bagley's descriptions of the situation over a period of nearly twenty years were put to the test when the shortage of competent and well-trained specialists was discovered during and after World War II and proved to be well founded.[53]

Bagley's theory of the curriculum, whether at the elementary or the secondary stage, aimed at imparting knowledge, not for its own sake, as he was frequently charged with believing, but for use and action, on the one side, and as background that would determine intelligent understanding of the world and standards of conduct. He rejected at all times the contemptuous use of the words "mere knowledge," because he refused to recognize any knowledge as "mere." A liberal or general education would enable its possessor to reduce the world to a measure of law, order, and system, and would also provide him with the general power to gain information independently and to adjust and adapt himself to new situations. By adaptability Bagley meant ability to apply past experience to the solution of new problems consciously, that is, by the use of judgment derived from past experience. Liberal education, he wrote in 1914, has recognized the importance of mastering certain units of knowledge representing large and important phases of human experience as an immediate aim but looking to remote ends. Vocational education develops specialized efficiency in some specialized occupation, while a liberal or cultural education cultivates adaptability to changing conditions.[54]

The frame of reference in Bagley's discussions of the sources of materials of education was always the experience of the race, or human experience, which constituted the social heritage of humanity. Facts and principles, ideas and meanings

> constitute one of the most important forms in which the experience of the race is crystallized, and, in virtue of the possibility of recording these resultants of experience in written and printed language, and in formulæ, diagrams, pictures, and models, facts and principles form numerically the largest class of educative materials.[55]

On the functional value of race experience Bagley made the following statement:

> But what is education for if it is not to preserve midst the chaos and confusion of troublous times the great truths that the race has wrung from its experience? . . . Is it not the specific task of education to represent in each generation the human experiences that have been tried and tested and found to work – to represent these in the face of opposition if need be – to be faithful to the trusteeship of the most priceless legacy that the past has left to the present and to the future?[56]

Subject matter became a term in dispute and to be "subject-conscious" was almost a scurrilous epithet. Bagley, however, considered subject matter primarily as the experience of the race. Direct personal experience through spontaneous activity he did not regard as a substitute "for that type of education which aims specifically to transmit to the learner those elements of the cultural heritage of mankind which give meaning and significance to the world in which we live and which have made possible some measure of control over natural forces."[57]

The following eloquent statement succinctly and in summary

form presents Bagley's approach to the curriculum and the materials of instruction and at the same time reflects the personality of its author.

> These materials form the common culture of our people. They are vastly more than instruments with which to do the day's work. They constitute the background and foundation of the Nation's life. They are at the roots of its ideals and aspirations. Upon them are based the standards with which our people as a whole evaluate the policies and programs of their leaders. Under the conditions of modern civilization, it is the universal school — the elementary school — that makes the nation what it is. There is no Hall of Fame that can compare for one moment with the curriculum of the elementary school in insuring immortality to the events, the feats, and the personalities that it includes. Everything that goes into this curriculum should be scrutinized, weighed, and evaluated with the last measure of patience, skill, insight, and devotion. There should be no place here for partisan bickerings or for unworthy compromises. There should be no place for snap judgments or cocksure opinions. But there is room in abundance for an attitude that must, I think, come to characterize our profession in a fundamental way — the attitude of serious humility in the face of a tremendous responsibility.[58]

In view of what has been written and documented up to this point it is difficult to understand why the world of American education seemed to be so taken by surprise when Bagley came out as the recognized leader of the Essentialist Movement in 1938. The proposal to start such a movement was initiated by Dr. F. Alden Shaw, principal of the Detroit Country Day School, and Dr. Michael J. Demiashkevich, professor of education at the George Peabody College for Teachers, Nashville, Tennessee. When the first meeting was held at Atlantic City in February 1938, Bagley was recognized as the leading exponent of essentialism in education, although he generously gave Dr. Demiashkevich credit for the use of the term "Essentialist" in his book, *An Introduction to the Philosophy of Education,* which was published in 1935.[59] It is an interesting sidelight on the times that Bagley's positive contributions to education — the preparation of teachers and a sound educational theory — were not nearly as well known by the students of education as his destructive criticisms of such trends in American education as determinism, education and crime, and progressive education, and other innovations. On the analogy of Molière's M. Buffon educators seem to have discovered only in 1938 that Bagley had always been talking essentialism. In his first book, *The Educative Process*, he wrote what the infant would lack without education "are the great essentials of human life that are transmitted, not directly through the germ cell, but indirectly by social contact — culture, 'education,' and civilized habits." In *Educational Values* he stated that "Thus the task of selecting for survival the essential elements of experience is one of the most troublesome constructive problems of the educator." He defined the essentials in *Craftsmanship in Teaching*, where he wrote that "Fundamentally the core of the elementary curriculum must, I believe, be the arts that are essential to everyone who lives the social life. In other words, the language arts and the number arts are, and always must be, the fundamentals of elementary education." To impart a pervasive common culture to all does not preclude the teaching of an abundance in nonessentials, he wrote in *Determinism in Education*.[60]

It is difficult to understand why the proponents of the progressive education movement were so disconcerted by the formation of the Essentialist Committee for the Advancement of American Education. An explanation may be found in the facts that their own leaders, John Dewey and Boyd H. Bode, had begun to be critical in the 'thirties of some of the trends that had appeared under the name of progressive education, that parents were beginning to question the results of that education, and that the Committee for the first time rallied together a group of educators who as individuals and each in his own way had expressed their opposition to the innovations under the banner of pragmatism, instrumentalism, or experimentalism. Fantastic charges were brought against the Essentialists — that in education they were like the fundamentalists in religion or like reactionaries in politics, and that they were inconspicuous people seeking notoriety because the new education was making such headway in the country. In a few years the contentions of the Essentialists were proved to be well founded, and the failure of the educational system, influenced by the progressive theories, to provide an intelligent and well-trained personnel for the Armed Forces during World War II and the years that followed strengthened their position. Sputnik did the rest.

The responsibility for defining the position of the Essentialist Committee fell on Bagley and in writing "An Essentialist's Platform for the Advancement of American Education" he brought together the criticisms that he had leveled throughout his career on innovations, hasty reforms, and progressive education, and presented his own philosophy of education as it had developed during the same period of time. He was writing at a critical period when the ideals of democracy were being challenged, when economic difficulties and problems of the country had to be met, and when the future of the world was endangered by the threat of war. All these aspects of the crisis prompted him to write that "it is particularly unfortunate that American education should be unnecessarily weak at a time when the situation at home and abroad is critical in the last degree." He was justified accordingly in concluding that

> hence a primary function of American education will be to safeguard and strengthen these ideals of American democracy, with especial emphasis upon freedom of speech, freedom of the press, freedom of assembly, and freedom of religion. It is clear enough now that whenever any one of these is permitted to collapse, the whole democratic structure will topple like a house of cards. These, then, are among the first essentials in the platform of the Essentialist.

This statement of the task that faced democracy on trial was prophetic not only of what happened a few years later, but also of what actually happened subsequently after Stalin and Khrushchev took the place of Hitler and Mussolini and after Soviet Russia launched Sputnik.

> Inevitably [wrote Bagley], the future will bring competition if not clashes and conflicts with the now militantly anti-democratic peoples. Democratic societies cannot survive either competition or conflict with totalitarian states unless there is a democratic discipline that will give

strength and solidarity to the democratic purpose and ideal. If the theory of democracy finds no place for discipline, then the theory will have before long only historic significance.

Accordingly, "a democratic society has a vital stake in the informed intelligence of every individual citizen." Discipline he stressed because he realized the contribution it could make "to the growth of volitional maturity" and as a stage to responsible freedom, always a conquest, never a gift.

When he turned his attention to the discussion of specifics Bagley put common learnings first, because "an effective democracy demands a community of culture. Educationally this means that each generation should be placed in possession of a common core of ideas, meanings, understandings, and ideals representing the most precious elements of the human heritage." The essentials, which he regarded as of the greatest importance, are the arts of recording, computing, and measuring — basic arts which have always been among the first concerns of organized education. To these he added a speaking acquaintance with man's past history and the history of one's own country. He held that "widening the space horizon and extending the time perspective are essential if the citizen is to be protected from the fallacies of the local and immediate." That the Essentialists were unfairly charged with advocating a static program of studies is clear from the statement that the social heritage and the essentials have been and will continue to be extended by investigation, invention, and creative art.

With specific reference to the United States Bagley wrote:

> A specific program of studies including these essentials should be the heart of a democratic system of education. In a country like ours with its highly mobile population there should be agreement as to the order and grade placement of subjects and especially of crucial topics. There is no valid reason for the extreme localism that has come to characterize American education. There is no valid reason for the failure of the American elementary school to lay as firm a foundation in the fundamentals of education as do the elementary schools of other democracies. It is especially regrettable that contemporary educational theory should in effect condone and rationalize scamped work by ridiculing such traits as thoroughness, accuracy, persistence, and

the ideal of good workmanship for its own sake. One may be sure that democracy schooled to the easy way will have short shrift in competition or conflict with any social order dominated by objectives which, however reprehensible, are clear-cut and appealing, and are consequently embraced even by disfranchised masses.

"But the essentials," he again pointed out, "should be taught as such through a systematic program of studies and activities for the carrying out of which the teachers must be responsible."

He foresaw what the results of the relaxation of standards would produce long before the leaders and the public discovered them during and after World War II. Pupils should be permitted to go at the pace their abilities permit and failure should not be stigmatized as in the past.

On the other hand, if education abandons rigorous standards and consequently provides no effective stimulus to the effort that learning requires, many persons will pass through twelve years of schooling only to find themselves in a world in which ignorance and lack of fundamental training are increasingly heavy handicaps. This in an all too true literal sense is to throw the baby out with the bath.

The final paragraph of what was generally considered the Manifesto of the Essentialist Committee might indeed have been written as a succinct digest of Bagley's philosophy of education:

A clear and primary duty of organized education at the present time is to recognize the fundamental changes that are already taking place, and to search diligently for means of counteracting their dangers. Let us repeat that an educational theory to meet these needs must be strong, virile, and positive, not feeble, effeminate, and vague. The theories that have increasingly dominated American education during the past generation are at basis distinctly of the latter type. The Essentialists have recognized and increasingly recognize the contributions of real value that these theories have made to educational practice. They believe, however, that these positive elements can be preserved in an educational theory which finds its basis in the necessary dependence of the immature upon the mature for guidance, instruction, and discipline. This dependence is inherent in human nature. "What has been ordained among the prehistoric protozoa," said Huxley, "cannot be altered by act of Parliament" — nor, we may add, by the wishful thinking of educational theorists, however sincere their motives. "Authoritarianism" is an ugly word. But when those who detest it carry their laudable rebellion against certain of its implications so far as to reject the authority of plain facts, their arguments, while well adapted perhaps to the generation of heat, become lamentably lacking in light.[61]

Although the Essentialist Committee did not undertake a strident campaign of propaganda and ceased to meet after 1942, its ends were achieved when a few years later the Progressive Education Association found occasion to change its name and subsequently ceased to exist. The public at large began to demand what Bagley had always referred to as a virile, vigorous, and rigorous education, and found leaders who came out for exact and exacting studies in secondary education. The indebtedness to Bagley or the Essentialists has never been acknowledged, however. Nevertheless, it is a great tribute to the man who for over forty years, and in the face of ridicule and opposition, stood consistently for a philosophy of education which was not starry-eyed, doctrinaire, and so vague as to prove itself to be unrealistic. Bagley's theory was based on insight into the needs of society and on the realities of the classroom. In his writings and in his professional career he lived up to his ideal of a democratic citizen. He described the principle that seems to have guided him throughout his career when he closed an address, which dealt, among other topics, with academic freedom, with these words: "There are occasions, when, with or without support or the prospect of support, one must stand firm — alone, if necessary, with one's back against the wall. That is the acid test both of conscience and of courage."[62]

CHAPTER 6

BAGLEY'S PLACE IN AMERICAN EDUCATION

DR. BAGLEY'S CLAIM TO A PROMINENT PLACE IN THE HISTORY of American education can be justified not on the ground that he was a reformer or innovator, but that, in the midst of a succession of innovations and new statements and definitions of educational aims, methods, and content, he was able to maintain a balanced point of view and a steady sense of direction. More than any of his contemporaries he was a worthy representative of the educational traditions of Horace Mann and Henry Barnard. His contributions to education were never sensational or spectacular, for he was a realist who understood the tasks with which the teacher in the classroom was confronted better than those who proclaimed doctrinaire panaceas and cure-alls which came out of a fertile imagination rather than out of familiarity with classroom experience. Because he realized that the man at the front — the teacher in the classroom — rather than the generalist or theoretician bore the responsibility for the progress and success of education, he was convinced that the strength of an educational system depended on the thorough preparation of the teacher. While others loudly proclaimed some revolutionary approach to the curriculum or advocated a patent method of instruction mainly from the point of view of the immedia felt needs of the pupils, Bagley was concerned chiefly that the teacher's initiative as a professional practitioner not be so restricted that he would be prevented from using the methods most appropriate to the varied situations that arise in a classroom.

Bagley's approach to curriculum matters was based on his conviction of the value and importance of a common cultural foundation for all, determined by the common needs and purposes of the society of which they are to become members. Beyond that, he considered that all subjects of the curriculum are representative of different phases of the universe of man and nature, which the human race has experienced and accumulated through the ages and preserved to meet its needs. He believed, further, that a general method, applicable to any subject, is impossible, and that each subject calls for the method most appropriate to it. The objection that his philosophy was static he anticipated when he wrote in his Preface to *Educational Values* that "the time will never be ripe for a final statement of values, for values vary with the varying conceptions of the end of education." He was as aware of the fact of social and cultural changes as those who built their theories upon them, but he did not make the mistake of confusing the superficial ripples with the permanent flow of the stream of human culture.

In his emphasis on the social aim of education he had in mind the responsibility of the school to the society that established it rather than a vague hope that the education of the individual in accordance with his own needs and interests and through the solution of problems would prepare him for the duties of citizenship. He felt that it was as important to cultivate a sense of discipline, responsibility, and duty as to stress the rights of the individual to freedom of self-determination and self-expression. He sought through reasoned discipline to lead up to self-discipline, and did not believe that obedience and loyalty were synonymous with the kind of indoctrination expected in an authoritarian system. He would have claimed that these educational ends represented unchanging values that were prerequisites to membership in society and made social living together possible. In the same spirit he was ready to justify the essentials of learning because their value lay in developing common understandings and a common language of discourse among the members of a society and contributed in that way to its security and stability. All these principles had their origin in Bagley's genetic approach, for he frequently repeated his major premise that the process of education is determined by the fact that it is intended to guide the immature to maturity and that a consciousness of intellectual needs emerges slowly and must be directed. In this process of guidance there must be a period in which provision is made for moral and intellectual disciplining. Instead of stressing freedom, as was done in the "dominant" theory from the start, Bagley proposed as a motto for education in a democracy "Through Discipline to Freedom."

The story of Essentialism is interesting and it is no discredit to Bagley and his colleagues in the movement to say that popular attention was directed to it by the attacks on it and on the Essentialist Committee by its opponents. For the opponents were more ruthless in their attacks on the movement, of which Bagley was recognized as the acknowledged leader, than Bagley ever was in his discussions of the opposing or what he called the "dominant" educational theory. To refer to Bagley as fundamentalist, reactionary, or inconspicuous was neither courteous nor a fair exchange for his recurring reference to the increments or contributions of the progressive movement. But modesty about his own work and generous tolerance of the views of others were notable characteristics of the man.

His patience was tried, however, when he felt that the new measures of intelligence were being put to wrong uses. The critical articles, which he began to write in the 'twenties, were not directed against the use of tests, as was generally and erroneously assumed, but against their misuse which might lead to social stratification through educational discrimination. In this campaign he took up the cause on behalf of the common man and stressed the educability of all as far as their potentialities would allow them to go. And in taking up the cause of the common man he did so because he saw in each an essential and potential member of society. He had greater faith in the collective wisdom of common men than in the leadership of a forceful personality. A sound education for the tasks of democracy should, he was convinced, prepare the masses of common men to choose their own leaders wisely. To use tests to discover who were intellectually worthy of selection to be educated as potential leaders and to ignore the rest would imply that those not so selected were not educable – a position that Bagley refused to accept as sound in a democracy. In so far as differences of intellectual capacity might be revealed by tests, they pointed, he believed, not to discrimination but to the adoption of methods of instruction appropriate to different types of ability. Differentiation might be introduced but only after all had acquired a common cultural foundation as the basis of mutual understanding.

That he did not ignore the existence of differences of mental ability became evident when, again in the 'twenties, Bagley began to criticize the generalists for disparaging and discrediting the academic subjects of the secondary school tradition and for depriving those who had the ability to pursue them of the opportunity to do so. Such a step, he felt, would mean ultimately a leveling down when the task of education should be to raise the intellectual level of the masses and to introduce as many pupils as possible to the traditional subjects. The "exact and exacting subjects," as he called them, did demand a certain type of ability, but the generalists, seeking to find subjects that would keep pupils in high schools as long as possible, reduced all studies to the same quantitative level and made a virtue of the cult of mediocrity. Nearly three decades before the academic specialists discovered what had happened, by their own default, to the subjects that they professed, Bagley had begun to plead on their behalf. He saw in this tendency to level down further evidence of the disparagement of the abilities of the common man and of the refusal to give the necessary attention to the development of appropriate methods of instruction instead of juggling with a multitude of subjects out of which programs could be tailor-made to suit each pupil's needs and interests.

It is perhaps illustrative of the attitude of the profession and of the public that the one innovation that Bagley hoped to bring about — the provision of a competent well-educated and well-prepared teacher in every classroom of the country's schools — has on the whole been ignored. Following his own recommendation that American educators should scrutinize the educational system for its weak and strong points and should direct their efforts to eliminating the weaknesses and extending the strong elements, he discovered early that the weakest link in the system was the preparation and status of teachers and the low esteem in which their occupation was held by the public. To the correction and elimination of these weaknesses he devoted most of the years of his active career. But for this devoted service Bagley never received adequate recognition. He came to be better known as the leader of the Essentialist Movement rather than as the chief protagonist for the improvement of the preparation of teachers, upon which the improvement of status would follow. Although the length of the preparation was extended gradually, his major recommendation of professionalized subject matter was either ignored or misunderstood. The conflict between academic subject-matter specialists and generalists or professors of education continued long after his death. The truce that he had hoped to bring about by injecting respect for subject matter and giving meaning to subjects as essential instruments of education in the preparation of teachers has not yet been generally effected. The field so long pre-empted by professors of education is beginning to be invaded by those who believe that this long-standing monopoly should be broken and that what they consider as the traditional overemphasis on professional courses should be curtailed.

Bagley had sounded a warning of this when in 1917 he expressed his conviction that much of the so-called "professional work is generally futile" because it was unrelated to other subjects. Professional preparation, he insisted, must include specific courses in subject matter organized from the standpoint of the specific problems of teaching. It is doubtful, however, whether he would have approved the current movement, financially stimulated, to stress the study of liberal arts subjects separately and then to "fasten the technology of teaching on them later," a practice which he often criticized.

If Bagley did not receive a full response to his theories and philosophy, except in the matter of discrimination in education, he did succeed in stimulating a large number of students through his personal influence and his readiness to be of service to them. When they came to his office at Teachers College, Columbia University, for example, a head would emerge from behind the screen of cigar smoke and a pile of books and Bagley would cheerfully welcome the visitors. For outstanding among his characteristics were his friendliness, his modesty, and his humility which immediately put students at their ease. On the platform he did not win adherents as a revivalist who played on the emotions of his listeners by offering a way of salvation to atone for the educational iniquities of the past, nor did he display any histrionic ability. But he did inspire his audiences with his integrity and sincerity and with his evident devotion to the cause of public education and of the teacher rather than through any tricks of oratory. In debate he was keen and formidable but he never descended to personalities. Although often chagrined by the antics and claims of his opponents, he tolerated them with good humor and maintained his unshaken confidence that he was right. This confidence was not a sign of arrogance but came from acting on a principle which he stated in 1939 and had inscribed on a plaque in his home: "If I cannot always be right, I will at least make a desperate effort always to be clear; for if I am clear and wrong, I can be corrected; but if I am obscure and wrong, people will merely think that I am wise." He always chose to be clear and right because he was always careful of his facts, and because he followed another of his maxims, to do as well as he could the task that his hand or head found to do.

Time proved him to have been right in most of his contentions. The ineffectual results of elementary education and the revelation during World War II of deficiencies in secondary and higher education caused an unrest, widespread among the public and academic leaders, and inspired the beginnings of a new era in American education to make the best of the traditional ideals and to salvage what Bagley thought had been the sound elements contributed by progressive education.

Bagley's place in the history of American education is assured not because he developed new theories but because of his sympathetic insight into the work and problems of the classroom teacher. He showed a sound and thorough understanding of the role of education in American society. He was a pioneer in bringing to the attention of teachers the contributions of the new psychology. Although he paid his respects to the science of education, he came to place greater emphasis on teaching as an art. The theory of education he always expounded in terms of its immediate practical implications rather than *ex cathedra*. Realizing that the strength of an educational system depends on the teachers, he devoted his attention to improving the quality of their preparation. In such preparation he believed that the major emphasis should be on giving the prospective teacher as rich a background of culture and scholarship as was expected in members of other professions, but this background should be given with a slant on the professional use to be made of it in the classroom. His faith in democracy was expressed in his faith in the educability of the common man, on whose behalf he undertook his critical attack on the abuse of intelligence tests. And in the same vein he insisted that the common interests in a nation or society demanded a common foundation of culture for all its members.

Before he reached the age of thirty Bagley had already formulated a design for living. He was fortunate in being able to see the pattern of this design unfold to the end of his life. The design he entitled "My Kingdom," a poem published in *Harper's* (Volume 103, 1902, page 341), the only poem of his which is on record.

My Kingdom

For this is my Kingdom: My peace with my neighbor,
The clasp of a hand or the warmth of a smile,
The sweetness of toil as the fruit of my labor —
The glad joy of living and working the while;
The birds and the flowers and the blue skies above me,
The green of the meadows, the gold of the grain,
A song in the evening, a dear heart to love me —
And just enough pleasure to balance the pain.

ACKNOWLEDGMENTS

THE AUTHOR IS INDEBTED TO THE PUBLISHERS OF THE BOOKS and the editors of the journals cited in the following pages for permission to quote from their publications, and to

William C. Bagley, Jr., who holds the copyrights of his father's works published by The Macmillan Company, New York

Eleanor L. Buchholz of Warwick & York, Inc., Baltimore, Maryland

Carnegie Foundation for the Advancement of Teaching
Classical Journal
Educational Method
Henry Holt & Co., Inc., New York
Journal of Geography
The Macmillan Company, New York
The Mathematics Teacher
National Education Association, Publications Division
The Ronald Press Company, New York
Philip A. Schilpp
Charles Scribner's Sons, New York
University of Minnesota Press, Minneapolis, Minnesota

REFERENCES

CHAPTER 1

1. *Educational Administration and Supervision,* Vol. 22, 1936, pp. 427 ff. (Warwick & York, Inc., Baltimore, Md.)
2. *Educational Administration and Supervision,* Vol. 27, 1941, pp. 161 ff.
3. *The Mathematics Teacher,* Vol. 28, 1938, p. 176.
4. N.E.A. *Proceedings,* 1914, p. 164.
5. *Craftsmanship in Teaching,* p. 127. (The Macmillan Company, New York, 1912.)
6. In a letter to Dr. Arthur B. Moehlman, December 12, 1944.
7. Hall-Quest, Alfred L., *Kappa Delta Pi, 1911–1936,* p. 123. (The Macmillan Company, New York, 1938.)
8. *Ibid.,* p. 344.
9. *The Educational Forum,* Vol. XI, January 1947, pp. 133 f.
10. University of Illinois School of Education, *Bulletin,* Vol. XIII, No. 16.
11. *Education, Crime, and Social Progress,* p. vii. (The Macmillan Company, New York, 1932.)
12. *A Century of the Universal School,* pp. xi f. (The Macmillan Company, New York, 1937.)
13. Bagley, W. C., and Thomas Alexander, *The Teacher of the Social Studies,* p. xii. (Charles Scribner's Sons, New York, 1937.)
14. "The School of the Air," *Educational Administration and Supervision,* Vol. 17, 1931, pp. 412 ff. See also "What the Future Holds for Broadcasting in the Schools," *School and Society,* Vol. 33, May 30, 1931, pp. 713 ff.
15. *School and Society,* Vol. 58, June 6, 1942, p. 639.

16. *Educational Administration and Supervision,* Vol. 19, 1933, p. 561.
17. *Educational Method,* Vol. 12, 1932–33, p. 495.
18. *Ibid.*, pp. 497 f.
19. "Modern Educational Theories and Practical Considerations," *School and Society,* Vol. 37, April 1, 1933, pp. 409 ff.

CHAPTER 3

1. *Craftsmanship in Teaching,* p. 128.
2. N.E.A. *Proceedings,* 1914, p. 162.
3. "Projects and Purposes in Teaching and in Learning," *Teachers College Record,* Vol. 22, 1921, p. 294.
4. *Classroom Management,* pp. 2 f. (The Macmillan Company, New York, 1907.)
5. *Ibid.*, pp. 13 f.
6. *Craftsmanship in Teaching,* pp. 77 f.
7. *Ibid.*, p. 127. See also pp. 120 and 220 on the same topic.
8. *Education, Crime, and Social Progress,* p. x.
9. *Ibid.*, p. 67.
10. *Education and Emergent Man,* p. 197. (The Ronald Press Company, New York, 1934.)
11. Comments on Dr. Cox's Editorial. *Educational Method,* Vol. 12, 1932–33, p. 499.
12. *Craftsmanship in Teaching,* p. 189.
13. N.E.A. *Proceedings,* 1917, p. 54.
14. *A Century of the Universal School,* p. 79.
15. *Educational Values,* p. 61. (The Macmillan Company, New York, 1911.)
16. *Education, Crime, and Social Progress,* p. 31.
17. *Education,* Vol. 63, 1943, p. 3.
18. See "Education and Our Democracy," *School and Society,* Vol. 8, August 31, 1918, pp. 341 ff.; "The Place of Duty and Discipline in a Democratic Scheme of Education," *Teachers College Record,* Vol. 19, pp. 419 ff.; and N.E.A. *Proceedings,* 1921, pp. 618 ff.
19. KEITH, JOHN A. H. and W. C. BAGLEY, *The Nation and the Schools,* p. 7. (The Macmillan Company, New York, 1920.)
20. N.E.A. *Proceedings,* 1918, p. 386. See also N.E.A. *Proceedings,* 1915, pp. 766 ff., and 1919, pp. 499 ff.

21. *Education and Emergent Man,* p. 131.
22. "A Federal Department of Education: Some Arguments *Pro* and *Con," Educational Administration and Supervision,* Vol. 22, 1936, p. 266.
23. *A Century of the Universal School,* p. 63.
24. N.E.A. *Proceedings,* 1914, pp. 161 ff.
25. *Ibid.,* p. 170.
26. "The Upward Expansion of Mass Education: Its Causes and Some of the Problems It Has Raised," in P. A. Schilpp, edr., *Higher Education Faces the Future,* p. 147. (Liveright Publishing Corp., New York, 1930.)
27. "Does the Junior College Movement Involve Unique Teaching Problems?" *Educational Administration and Supervision,* Vol. 24, 1938, p. 339.
28. N.E.A. *Proceedings,* 1921, pp. 694 f.
29. "Illiteracy and Near-Illiteracy in the Selective Age Groups," *School and Society,* Vol. 58, June 6, 1942, p. 639.
30. *Education and Emergent Man,* pp. 106 f.
31. The preceding pages are based on *Determinism in Education: A Series of Papers on the Relative Influence of Inherited and Acquired Traits in Determining Intelligence, Achievement, and Character,* from which the quotations are taken. (Warwick & York, Inc., Baltimore, Md., 1925.)
32. "An Essentialist's Platform for the Advancement of Education," *Educational Administration and Supervision,* Vol. 24, 1938, p. 251.
33. "Guidance Programs During and Following the War," *Educational Administration and Supervision,* Vol. 28, 1942, p. 36.

CHAPTER 4

1. Keith, John A. H., and W. C. Bagley, *The Nation and the Schools,* Ch. XIX.
2. Judd, C. H., and S. C. Parker, "Problems Involved in Standardizing State Normal Schools," U.S. Bureau of Education, *Bulletin,* 1916, No. 12, p. 137.
3. "The Teacher's Contribution to Modern Progress," *The Teachers' Journal and Abstract,* Vol. 4, 1929, p. 453.

4. "Basic Problems of Teacher Education," *Teacher-Educational Journal,* Vol. I, 1938, p. 101.
5. CARNEGIE FOUNDATION, *The Professional Preparation of Teachers for American Public Schools,* p. 149 (New York, 1918).
6. "The Distinction between Academic and Professional Subjects," N.E.A. *Proceedings,* 1918, pp. 229 ff. It is interesting that the issue has been recognized in the preparation for another profession. Lord Horder, writing in the *British Medical Journal,* 1951, p. 1359, said: "The anatomy, the physiology, the chemistry, and the physics of the preclinical studies of the medical student should be directed towards the actual examination of the patient. I think we took a step backwards when we put the academic anatomist, physicist, and the chemist in charge of preclinical studies. These men staked out large claims for their respective spheres as though medical students were in training for professorships in these subjects rather than being doctors in embryo. This view led me to plead for less time spent over the latest structure of the organ of Corti and the theories of color vision, and more time over . . . simple instruments by which the structure and function of the normal body are studied. . . . I still meet doctors who have never seen the optic disk clearly, nor the vocal cords at all."
7. "Twenty Years Progress in the Professionalization of Subject-Matter in Normal Schools and Teachers Colleges," N.E.A. *Proceedings,* 1928, pp. 906 f.
8. *Ibid.,* p. 911.
9. BAGLEY, WILLIAM C., and THOMAS ALEXANDER, *The Teacher of the Social Studies,* pp. 44 f.
10. "The Control of Educational Progress through Professional Progress," N.E.A. *Proceedings,* 1917, p. 205.
11. "The Element of Adventure in Teaching and Learning Geography," *Journal of Geography,* Vol. 28, March 1929, p. 90.
12. "Teaching as a Fine Art," N.E.A. *Proceedings,* 1930, p. 789.
13. *Education and Emergent Man,* pp. 194 f.
14. "The Future of American Education," *School and Society,* Vol. 32, July 5, 1930, p. 5.
15. "The Teacher's Contribution to Modern Progress," *The Teachers' Journal and Abstract,* Vol. 4, 1929, p. 449.
16. *Classroom Management,* p. 273.
17. BAGLEY and ALEXANDER, *op. cit.,* p. 9. See also BAGLEY, "The

Profession of Teaching in the United States," *School and Society,* Vol. 29, January 26, 1929, pp. 101 ff.; and "The University School as a Source of Educational Leadership," in A. L. EURICH, edr., *The Changing Educational World,* pp. 79 ff. (University of Minnesota Press, Minneapolis, Minn., 1931.)

18. In EURICH, *op. cit.*, p. 81.
19. See BAGLEY, "Professors of Education and Their Academic Colleagues," *The Mathematics Teacher,* Vol. 23, 1930, pp. 277 ff; and "The Upward Expansion of Mass Education: Its Causes and Some of Its Problems," in P. A. SCHILPP, edr., *Higher Education Faces the Future,* pp. 135 ff.
20. "Twenty Years Progress in the Professionalization of Subject-Matter in Normal Schools and Teachers Colleges," N.E.A. *Proceedings,* 1928, p. 906.
21. In EURICH, *op. cit.*, pp. 83 f.
22. "The Element of Adventure in Teaching and Learning Geography," *Journal of Geography,* Vol. 28, March 1929, p. 89.
23. "The Status of the Classroom Teacher," N.E.A. *Proceedings,* 1918, p. 384.
24. 'The Profession of Teaching in the United States," *School and Society,* Vol. 29, January 26, 1929, p. 109.
25. See CARNEGIE FOUNDATION, *The Professional Preparation of Teachers for American Public Schools,* 1918, p. 137; "The Status of the Classroom Teacher," N.E.A. *Proceedings,* 1918, p. 384; and "Professionalism in Education," *Teachers College Record,* Vol. 26, 1924, p. 6.

CHAPTER 5

1. *Craftsmanship in Teaching,* p. 127.
2. *Education, Crime, and Social Progress,* p. 91.
3. Osborn's "Foreword" to F. TILNEY and H. A. RILEY, *The Brain from Ape to Man* (Paul B. Hoeber, Inc., New York, 1928).
4. *Education, Crime, and Social Progress,* p. 112.
5. *Education and Emergent Man,* p. 1. Italics in original.
6. *Ibid.*, pp. 20 and 22 f., respectively.
7. *The Educative Process,* pp. 107–109 and 263, respectively. Italics in the original. (The Macmillan Company, New York, 1905.)

8. *Educational Values,* p. 61. See also p. 138 where the effect of material prosperity on education is again discussed.
9. *Craftsmanship in Teaching,* p. 69.
10. *Education, Crime, and Social Progress,* pp. 33 f. Italics in the original.
11. "The Significance of the Essentialist Movement in Educational Theory," *Classical Journal,* Vol. 34, 1938–39, pp. 343 f.
12. *A Century of the Universal School,* p. 64.
13. "Some Handicaps of Character Education in the United States," N.E.A. *Proceedings,* 1929, p. 767.
14. "The Upward Expansion of Mass Education: Its Causes and Some of the Problems It Has Raised," in P. A. SCHILPP, edr., *Higher Education Faces the Future,* p. 147.
15. *Education, Crime, and Social Progress,* p. xi.
16. *The Educative Process,* pp. 61 f.
17. *Educational Values,* pp. 15 and 60, respectively.
18. *Craftsmanship in Teaching,* p. 166.
19. *Classroom Management,* pp. 273 f.
20. "The Place of Duty and Discipline in a Democratic Scheme of Education," *Teachers College Record,* Vol. 19, 1918, p. 419.
21. *School Discipline,* p. 240. (The Macmillan Company, New York, 1914.)
22. *Determinism in Education,* pp. 26 and 34, respectively.
23. *Education, Crime, and Social Progress,* pp. 5 and 83.
24. "An Essentialist's Program for the Advancement of American Education," *Educational Administration and Supervision,* Vol. 24, April 1938, pp. 251 f. See also *School and Society,* Vol. 61, June 30, 1945, p. 422.
25. "The Teacher's Contribution to Modern Progress," *The Teachers' Journal and Abstract,* Vol. 4, 1929, pp. 447 f.
26. "Progressive Education Is Too Soft," *Education,* Vol. 60, October 1939, p. 78.
27. *Educational Values,* pp. 107 and 110, respectively.
28. *The Educative Process,* p. 65.
29. *Education and Emergent Man,* p. 126.
30. *Educational Values,* Chapters IV and XI.
31. *Craftsmanship in Teaching,* pp. 113 f.
32. *Education and Emergent Man,* pp. 76 f.
33. *The Educative Process,* pp. 93 and 103, respectively. Italics in the original.

34. *Education, Crime, and Social Progress,* p. 107. Italics in the original.
35. *School Discipline,* p. 239. Italics in the original.
36. See "What Is the Crux between the Progressives and the Essentialists?" *Educational Administration and Supervision,* Vol. 26, 1940, pp. 508 ff.; "Modern Educational Theories and Practical Considerations," *School and Society,* Vol. 37, April 1, 1933, p. 410; and "How Shall We View Elementary Education as Regards (1) Discipline; (2) Psychology of Learning; (3) Subject Matter?" *Mathematics Teacher,* Vol. 28, March 1935, p. 168.
37. "Is Subject-Matter Obsolete?" *Educational Administration and Supervision,* Vol. 21, 1935, p. 404.
38. *School Discipline,* p. 8.
39. "The Crucial Problem for the Next Decade," *Journal of the N.E.A.,* Vol. 18, 1929, p. 108; and "Some Handicaps of Character Education in the United States," N.E.A. *Proceedings,* 1929, p. 738.
40. *Determinism in Education,* p. 160.
41. "Progressive Education Is Too Soft," *Education,* Vol. 60, October 1939, p. 81.
42. *Classroom Management,* p. 14.
43. "How Shall We View Elementary Education, etc.," *Mathematics Teacher,* Vol. 28, March 1935, pp. 179 f.
44. *The Educative Process,* p. 38.
45. *Craftsmanship in Teaching,* p. 97.
46. *Ibid.,* p. 145.
47. *Ibid.,* pp. 177 f.
48. "The Yearbook on the Teaching of Geography from the Point of View of a Student of Geography," *Journal of Geography,* Vol. 32, April 1933, p. 160.
49. "Progressive Education Is Too Soft," *Education,* Vol. 60, October 1939, p. 77.
50. "What Should Be the Equipment in Natural Sciences of Teachers in Other Fields?" *Educational Administration and Supervision,* Vol. 24, 1938, p. 564.
51. N.E.A. *Proceedings,* 1929, p. 767.
52. "What Should Be the Equipment, etc.?" *Educational Administration and Supervision,* Vol. 24, 1938, p. 562.
53. See "The Upward Expansion of Mass Education: Its Causes and Some of Its Problems," in P. A. SCHILPP, edr., *Higher Education*

Faces the Future, pp. 135 ff. (New York, 1930); "The Significance of the Essentialist Movement in Educational Theory," *Classical Journal*, Vol. 34, 1938–39, pp. 1331 ff.; "An Essentialist Looks at Foreign Languages," *Educational Administration and Supervision*, Vol. 25, 1939, pp. 241 ff.; "Guidance Programs During and Following the War," *ibid.*, Vol. 28, 1942, pp. 81 ff.; "Progressive Education Is Too Soft," *Education*, Vol. 60, 1939, pp. 76 ff.

54. N.E.A. *Proceedings*, 1914, pp. 161 ff.
55. *Educational Values*, p. 47.
56. *Craftsmanship in Teaching*, p. 119.
57. "How Shall We View Elementary Education, etc.?" *Mathematics Teacher*, Vol. 28, March 1935, p. 170.

    On the issue of race experience it is difficult to see any profound difference between Bagley's position and that of John Dewey in a passage which seems to have been overlooked by his disciples. In *Human Nature and Conduct*, Dewey wrote, "It is of grace not of ourselves that we lead civilized lives. . . . Loyalty to whatever in the established environment makes a life of excellence possible is the beginning of all progress. The best we can accomplish for posterity is to transmit unimpaired and with some increment of meaning the environment that makes it possible to maintain the habit of a decent and refined life. Our individual habits are links in forming the endless chain of humanity. Their significance depends upon the environment inherited from our forefathers, and it is enhanced as we foresee the fruits of our labors in the world in which our successors live.

    "For however much has been done, there always remains more to do. We can retain and transmit our own heritage only by constantly remaking our own environment. Piety to the past is not for its own sake nor for the sake of the past, but for the sake of a present so secure and enriched that it will create a yet better future." (Henry Holt & Co., Inc., New York, 1922, pp. 21 f.)
58. "Professionalism in Education," *Teachers College Record*, Vol. 26, 1924–1925, p. 12.
59. Pp. 5 f.
60. The critics of Bagley's position on common learnings, essentialism, and transmission of race experience need to be reminded that on this point the difference between Bagley and Dewey was hardly noticeable. For in *Democracy and Education*, Dewey wrote: "All

information and systematized scientific subject matter have been worked out under the conditions of social life and have been transmitted by social means. But this does not prove that all is of equal value for the purpose of forming the disposition and supplying the equipment of members of present society. The scheme of a curriculum must take account of the adaptation of studies to the needs of the existing community life; it must select with the intention of improving the life we live in common so that the future shall be better than the past. Moreover, *the curriculum must be planned with reference to placing essentials first and refinements second.* The things which are socially most fundamental, that is, which have to do with the experiences in which the widest groups share, are the essentials." (The Macmillan Company, New York, 1916, p. 225; italics not in the original.)

61. Quotations are from "An Essentialist's Platform for the Advancement of American Education," *Educational Administration and Supervision,* Vol. 24, April 1938, pp. 250 ff. For other articles by Bagley on the theme of essentialism, see note 53 above.
62. "Teachers' Rights, Academic Freedom, and the Teaching of Controversial Issues," *Teachers College Record,* Vol. 40, November 1938, p. 108.